Ayrsl Street

CW00741440

CONTENTS

Area of coverage & key to map symbols	2 - 3
Ardrossan, Saltcoats, Stevenston & index	4 - 9
Annbank, Mossblown & index	10 - 11
Ayr & Alloway	12 - 17
Auchinleck, Ballantrae, Barr, Barrhill & indices	18 - 19
Beith, Bellsbank & indices	20 - 21
Catrine, Colmonell, Coylton & indices	22 - 23
Crookedholm, Crosshill, Crosshouse, Knockentiber & indices	24 - 25
Cumnock, Dailly, Dalrymple & indices	26 - 29
Dalmellington, Drongan & indices	30 - 31
Dalry, Dunlop & indices	32 - 33
Darvel, Drybridge, Dundonald & indices	34 - 35
Fairlie, Fenwick, Hillhead & indices	36 - 37
Galston, Girvan & indices	38 - 39
Hurlford & index, Irvine (includes Dreghorn & Springside)	40 - 49
Kilbirnie (includes Glengarnock), Kirkmichael, Kilmaurs & indices	50 - 53
Kilmarnock & index	54 - 61
Kilwinning	62 - 63
Kirkoswald, Largs, Logan, Lugar & indices	64 - 67
Mauchline, Maidens & indices	68 - 69
Maybole, Minishant & indices	70 - 71
Millport & index	72 - 73
Muirkirk & index	74 - 75
New Cumnock & index	76 - 77
Newmilns, Ochiltree, Sorn & indices	78 - 79
Prestwick, Monkton & indices	80 - 83
Patna, Skelmorlie & indices	84 - 85
Stewarton, Symington & indices	86 - 87
Tarbolton, Troon (includes Barassie) & indices	88 - 91
Turnberry & index, West Kilbride & Seamill	92 - 93
Index section:	
West Kilbride & Seamill	94
Ayr (includes Alloway)	94 - 96
Irvine (includes Dreghorn & Springside)	96 - 99
Kilwinning	99

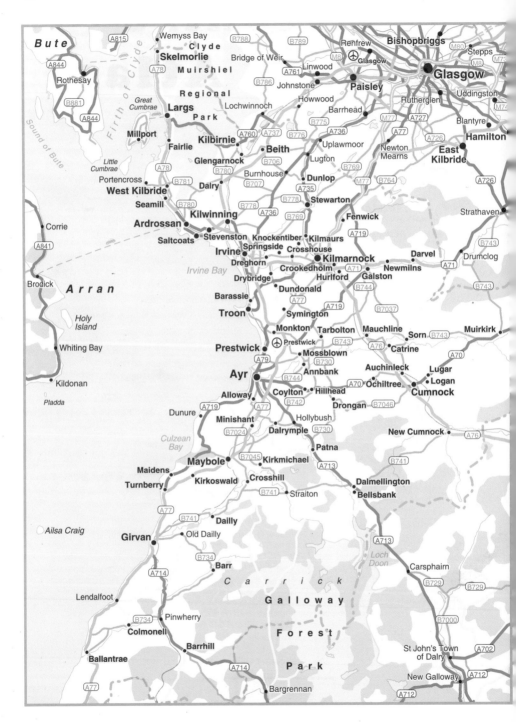

M77	Motorway	PO	Post office
A75	Primary route dual / single	S	Superstore
A79	A road dual / single	B	Bus station
B707	B road dual / single	i	Tourist information centre
	Unclassified road	a	Antiquity
	Pedestrianised road	m	Museum
	Track / path		Castle
	Historic wall		Historic or visitable house
	Railway / tunnel or disused rail		Battlefield
	Railway station		Garden
	Airport / heliport		Caravan site
▲	Primary school		Camping
▼	Secondary school		Viewpoint
△	Special or independent school		Other tourist attraction
	Police station	+	Church or place of worship
	Fire station		Woodland
	Ambulance station		Park, recreation, sports or cemetery
	Lifeboat station		Built up area
	Coastguard station		Rocks
H	Hospital		Shingle
P	Parking		Sand
F	Filling station		Marshland
L	Library		Loch

Scale 1:14 000

0 — 500m

0 — 500yds

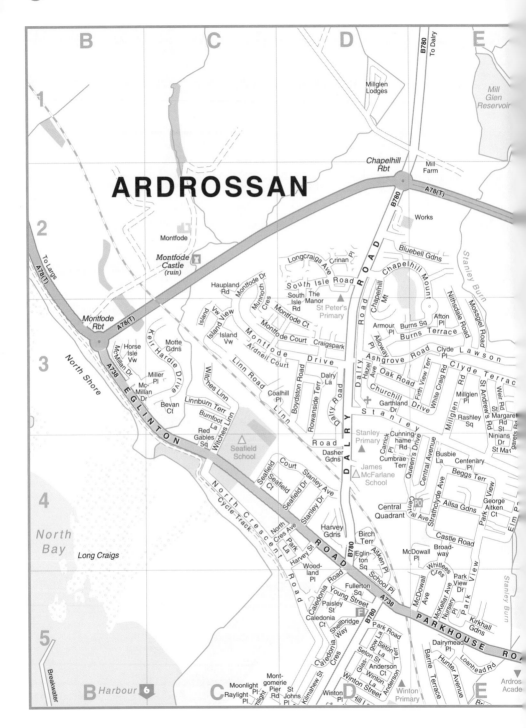

F   G   H   J

1

West
Knockrivoch
Mount

Knockrivoch

East
Knockrivoch
Mount

Sorbie

To Dalry
B714

2

Sorbie Road

South
Knockrivoch
Mount

A78(T)

Sharphill
Rbt

B714

To Stevenston & Kilwinning
A78(T)

3

Whitlees

Knockrivoch
Wynd

Sharphill
Mast

Dykesmains

Knock-
rivoch
Gdns

Knockrivoch Pl

Sorbie

Road

reenacres

Betsy
Miller Wynd
Spindrift Wynd

Clytus
Ct

St
Andrews
Ct

Barga Gardens

Sharphill
Industrial
Estate

Middlepart

Auchanshangan Dr

Weavers
Way
Wilson
Pl
Salters
Way
Allan
Gdns

Dunbar
Gdns

Kenneth
Campbell
Pl

Farm-
hill
Pl

Keeper
Pl

White
Pl

Bryson
Pl

4

Moffat Wynd

Deny
Ave

Garrett

Dykesmains
Primary

Meiklelaight Pl

sandmill

Carrick Avenue

White
Wynd

Burns

Ave

Crescent

Knock
Jargon Ct

Carey
Rd

Lochlea
Rd

Fleming Cres

Road

Burns

Hilton Ct
Kemp Ct
Murdoch
Ct

Lennox
Wynd

Lands-
borough
Ct

Simpson
Dr

Doon Pl

Mossgiel
Pl

Ellisland
Pl

Dalry

Martin
Sq

Mulgrew Ave

Corsankell
Wynd

Caff
Water
Pl

Three
Sisters
Ct

Corrie

Cumbrae Rd

Sanda

Islay
Cres

Davaar Road

Fleming Crescent

Duff Pl

Boyd Orr Rd

Jean
Armour
Pl

Keir
Hardie

Abbots-
ford Pl

Kenilworth Dr

Road

Longfield Place

Kilmory Rd

Crescent

Ashdale
Ave

Avenue

Wheatley
Rd

Talisman
Wk

Munro
Wk

Mayfield
Primary

Longfield Ave

Pirnmill Rd

Dippin Pl

Catacol
Ave

Kildonan
Pl

Rosa Pl

Wheatley
Gdns

Place

Primrose
Pl

James
Reid
School

Mid Dykes Road

Murray Avenue

Kilbrannan
Ave

Pladda Road

Ross Road

Sannox

Drive

Arran
Pl

Shaw
Pl

Gilfillan

Drive

Hogarth
Pl

Dykesfield
Pl

Springvale Nursery

Loch-
wood
Gdns

Saughtree

Lochranza
Pl

Fleck Ave

7

J

HIGH ROAD

Links

McKillon

Dykes

McGillivray

McKinnon
Pl

Clark

New England

Mayfield

F   G   H   J

St Anthony's
Primary

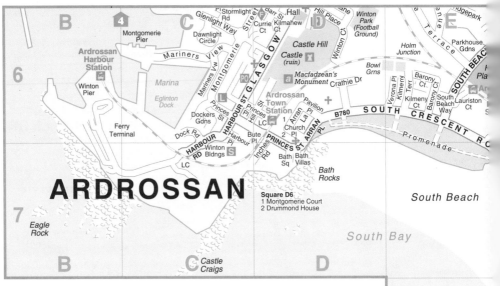

ARDROSSAN

Square D6
1 Montgomerie Court
2 Drummond House

South Beach

South Bay

Eagle Rock

Castle Craigs

West Shore

Index to Ardrossan

Abbotsford Place	H5	Baberton Way	Q4	Byrehill Drive	P5		
Adair Avenue	G6	Barga Gardens	G4	Byrehill Place	Q5		
Adams Avenue	G6	Barnett Court	G8	Caff Water Place	F5		
Acids Road	Q10	Barnett Crescent	G8	Caledonia Court	D5		
Afton Court	L7	Barony Court	E6	Caledonia Crescent	D5		
Afton Place	E3	Barr Street	D6	Caledonia Road	D5		
Afton Road	L6	Barra Place	N5	(Ardrossan)			
Ailsa Drive	K7	Barrie Terrace	E5	Caledonia Road	F6, F7		
Ailsa Gardens	E4	Bath Square	D7	(Saltcoats)			
Ailsa Road	H6	Bath Villas	D7	Caledonian Road	M8		
Aitken Place	D4	Beattie Court	L8	Caley Court	L8		
Alexander Avenue	M5	Beggs Terrace	E4	Cambuskeith Road	M4		
Alexander Place	L6	Berchem Place	G7	Campbell Avenue	F7		
Allan Gardens	G4	Betsy Miller Wynd	G4	(Saltcoats)			
Alloway Place	D3	Bevan Court	C3	Campbell Avenue	L5		
Anderson Court	D5	Birch Place	D4	(Stevenston)			
Anderson Drive	H5, H6	Blakely Road	J8	Canal Court	H8		
Anderson Terrace	D5	Bluebell Gardens	E2	Canal Crescent	L8		
Ardchoille Drive	M5	Boglemart Street	K7	Canal Place	H8		
Ardchoille Lane	M5	Bonnie Lesley Court	L7	Canal Street	H8		
Ardeer Lane	N9	Border Avenue	G7	Caponcraig Avenue	K6		
Ardlui Terrace	H7	Border Place	G7	Carey Road	G4		
Ardneil Court	C3	Boyd Orr Road	H5	Carment Drive	M8	Clyde Terrace	E
Ardoch Court	M9	Boydston Road	D3	Carmyle Place	L8	Clyde View Avenue	K
Ardoch Crescent	M9	Bradshaw Street	G8	Carrick Avenue	H4	Clytus Court	G
Ardoch Terrace	M8	Braehead Lane	G7	Carrick Place	D4	Coalhill Place	C
Ardrossan Road	F7	Braehead Place	G7	Castle Avenue	M5	Corrie Crescent	G
Argyle Place	F7	Braes Road	F8	Castle Road	E4	Corsankell Wynd	F
Argyle Road	G7	Bridgepark	E6	Castlehill Farm	P4	Countess Street	G
Armour Place	D3	Broadway	E4	Castlehill Road	N5	Craigdene Drive	M
Arran Court	K7	Brown Place	F6	Catacol Avenue	G5	Craigs Place	H
Arran Lane	D6	Bryson Place	H4	Centenary Place	E4	Craigspark	D
Arran Place (Ardrossan)	D6	Burma Road	P10	Central Avenue	E4	Crathie Drive	D
Arran Place (Saltcoats)	H5	Burn Road	E7	(Ardrossan)		Crinan Place	D
Arthur Street (Saltcoats)	H8	Burnbank Street	L7	Central Avenue	P10	Cumbrae Road	G
Arthur Street	L7	Burnfoot Lane	C3	(Stevenston)		Cumbrae Terrace	D
(Stevenston)		Burnlea Place	M5	Central Quadrant	D4	Cunninghame Crescent	H
Arthurlie Place	F7	Burns Avenue	F4, G4	Chapelwell Street	G8	Cunninghame Drive	J
Ashdale Avenue	G5	Burns Place	M6	Chaplehill Mount	D2	Cunninghame Road	D
Ashgrove Avenue	M5	Burns Square	E3	Chapelhill Road	D3	(Ardrossan)	
Ashgrove Road	D3	Burns Terrace	D3	Christie Gardens	G7	Cunninghame Road	H
Auchanshangan Drive	F4	Burnside Place	L6	Church Place	D6	(Saltcoats)	
Auchenharvie Place	J6	Busbie Lane	E4	Churchill Drive	D3	Currie Court	D
Auchenharvie Road	H7	Bute Court	K7	Clark Crescent	L8	Dairymead Place	E
		Bute Place	C7	Clark Place	H5	Dalry Lane	D
		Bute Terrace	F6	Clements Place	M5	Dalry Road (Ardrossan)	D
				Clyde Place	E3		

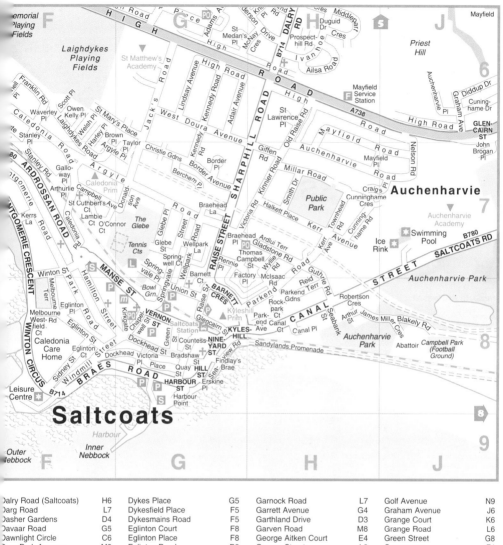

Saltcoats

Auchenharvie

Dalry Road (Saltcoats)	H6	Dykes Place	G5	Garnock Road	L7	Golf Avenue	N9
Darg Road	L7	Dykesfield Place	F5	Garrett Avenue	G4	Graham Avenue	J6
Dasher Gardens	D4	Dykesmains Road	F5	Garthland Drive	D3	Grange Court	K6
Davaar Road	G5	Eglinton Court	F8	Garven Road	M8	Grange Road	L6
Dawnlight Circle	C6	Eglinton Place	F8	George Aitken Court	E4	Green Street	G8
Deer Park Avenue	M8	Eglinton Road	B3	George Street	L8	Greenacres	F4
Denny Crescent	G4	Eglinton Square	D4	Giffen Road	H7	Greenhead Avenue	M5
Diddup Drive	J6	Eglinton Street	F8	Gilfillan Avenue	H5	Guthrie Road	H7
Dippin Place	G5	Ellisland Place	H4	Gilmour Wynd	M6	Halkett Place	H7
Dock Road	C6	Elm Park	E4	Gladstone Road	H7	Hamilton Crescent	N5
Dockers Gardens	C6	Elms Place	M5	Glasgow Lane	D5	Hamilton Street	F8
Dockhead Place	G8	Erskine Place	G8	Glasgow Street	D6	Harbour Place	C6
Dockhead Street	G8	Factory Place	G7	Glebe Place	G7	Harbour Road	C7
Donaldson Avenue	G7	Farmhill Place	H4	Glebe Street (Saltcoats)	G7	Harbour Point	G8
(Saltcoats)		Findlays Brae	G8	Glebe Street (Stevenston)	K6	Harbour Street	C6
Donaldson Avenue	M5	First Avenue	N8	Glen Crescent	K6	(Ardrossan)	
(Stevenston)		Firth View Terrace	E3	Glencairn Gardens	L6	Harbour Street	G8
Doon Place	H4	Fleck Avenue	H5	Glencairn Street	G8	(Saltcoats)	
Dornoch Court	Q4	Fleming Crescent	H4	(Saltcoats)		Harley Place	F7
Drummond House (2)	D6	Forde Crescent	M5	Glencairn Street	K6	Harvey Gardens	D4
Dubbs Road	N6	Franklin Road	F6	(Stevenston)		Harvey Street	D4
Duff Place	H5	Fullerton Place	K7	Glencairn Terrace	L6	Haupland Road	C2
Duguid Drive	H6	Fullerton Square	D5	Glenlight Way	C6	Hawkhill Drive	N6
Dunbar Gardens	G4	Galloway Place	F7	Goldie Place	K6	continued overleaf....	

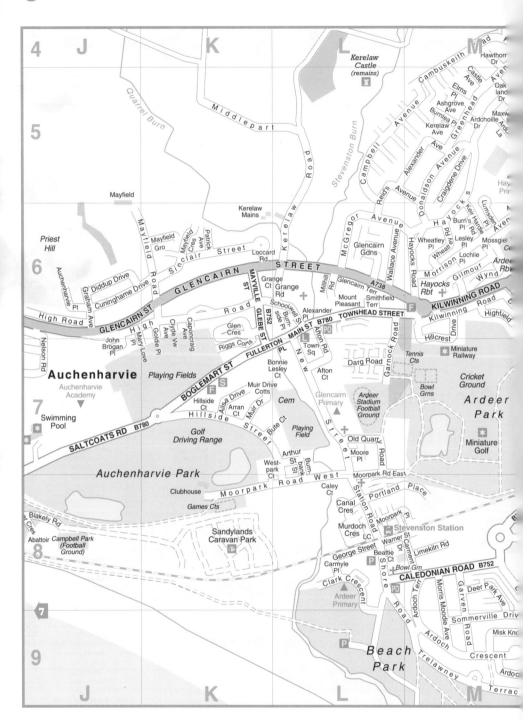

STEVENSTON

Kerelaw Castle (remains)

Middlepart Road

Quarrel Burn

Stevenston Burn

Kerelaw Mains

Mayfield

Priest Hill

Cambuskeith
Hawthorn Dr
Castle Ave
Oakland Dr
Elms Pl
Ashgrove Ave
Burnlea Pl
Kerelaw Ave
Maxw
Ardchoille Dr
Greenhead
Craigdene Drive
Donaldson Avenue

Campbell Avenue
Alexander Avenue
Reids Avenue
McGregor Avenue
Wallace Avenue

Hayocks
Burn's Pl
Wheatley Pl
Lesley Pl
Mossgiel Pl
Lochlie Pl
Morrison Pl
Gilmour
Hayocks Road
Ardee
Rbt

Glencairn Gdns

Kilsler
Keir Hardie
Hardie Pl
Ce
Wynd

Mayfield Road
Mayfield Gro
Mayfield Cres
Patrick Ave
Sinclair Street
Loccard Rd

GLENCAIRN STREET

Glencairn Terr
Mount Pleasant
Smithfield Terr
A738
KILWINNING ROAD
Kilwinning Road
Highfield

Auchenharvie Pl
Graham Ave
High Road
GLENCAIRN ST

Diddup Drive
Cuninghame Drive
MAYVILLE ST
Grange Ct
Grange Rd

Millhill Rd

Hayocks Rbt

Nelson Rd
High
Mary Love
Goldie Pl
Clyde Vw
John Brogan Pl
Caponcraig Ave
Riggs Cors

GLEBE ST
B752
Road
Glen Cres
Schoolwell St
Burn-side Pl
Alexander Pl
FULLERTON PL
MAIN ST
Afton Rd
B780
TOWNHEAD STREET

Hillcrest

Auchenharvie

Auchenharvie Academy

Swimming Pool

BOGLEMART ST

Playing Fields

F S
Hillside Ct
Ailsa Drive
Arran Ct
Muir Dr
Hillside Street
Bute Ct

Muir Drive Cotts

Cem

Town Sq
New Street
Afton Ct

Darg Road

Tennis Cts

Glencairn Primary

Ardeer Stadium Football Ground

Old Quarr

Moore Pl

Bowl Grns

Ardeer Park

Miniature Railway

Cricket Ground

Miniature Golf

SALTCOATS RD B780

Golf Driving Range

Playing Field

Arthur St

Westpark Ct
bank St
Burn St

West Road

Moorpark Rd East

Caley Ct

Portland Place

Garnock Road
Station Road
Moorpark Road

Auchenharvie Park

Clubhouse

Moorpark Road

Games Cts

Blakely Rd
Cres
Abattoir
Campbell Park (Football Ground)

Sandylands Caravan Park

Canal Cres
Murdoch Cres
George Street
Carmyle Pl
Clark Crescent

LC
Warner Pl
Beattie Ct
Bowl Grn
Limekiln Rd
St Carment

Stevenston Station

Ardeer Primary

Shore Road

CALEDONIAN ROAD B752

Ardoch Terr
Morris Moodie Ave
Ardoch Road
Garven Road
Deer Park Ave
Sommerville Driv
Misk Kno
Crescent
Ardoc
Terrac

Beach Park

Trelawney

PO

P

Stevenston

Pennyburn Roundabout

West Byrehill Industrial Estate

Hawkhill Retail Park

Stevenston Industrial Estate

Go-cart Track

Nicolson Maps

See inset

Greenacres Caravan Park

Ardeer Mains

Inset

Nobel Industrial Estate

continued from p.6...

Street	Grid
Hawkhill Place	N5
Hawthorn Drive	M4
Hayocks Road	M6
Hazel Avenue	D3
High Road	G6
Highfield Drive	M6
Hill Lane	D5
Hill Place	D6
Hill Street (Ardrossan)	D6
Hill Street (Saltcoats)	G8
Hillcrest Drive	M6
Hillhead Road	M4
Hillside Court	K7
Hillside Street	K7
Hilton Court	F4
Hogarth Avenue	F5
Horse Isle View	B3
Hunter Avenue	E5
Hyslop Road	N5
Inches Road	C7
Island View	C3
Islay Crescent	G5
Ivanhoe Drive	H6
Jacks Road	G6
James Miller Crescent	H8
Jean Armour Place	H4
John Brogan Place	J7
Keeper Place	H4
Keir Hardie Drive	C3
Keir Hardie Place	H5
Keir Hardie Road	M6
Kemp Court	F4
Kenilworth Drive	H5
Kennedy Road	G6
Kenneth Campbell Place	G4
Kerelaw Avenue	M5
Kerelaw Road	L6
Kerr Avenue	H7
Kerrs Lane	F7
Kilbrannan Avenue	G5
Kildonan Place	G5
Kilmahew Court	D6
Kilmahew Street	D5
Kilmeny Court	E6
Kilmeny Terrace	E6
Kilmory Road	G5
Kilwinning Road	M6
Kinnier Road	H7
Kirkgate	G8
Kirkhall Gardens	E5
Knock Jargon Court	F4
Knockrivoch Gardens	F3
Knockrivoch Place	F3
Knockrivoch Wynd	F3
Knox Place	H6
Kyleshill	G8
Laighdykes Road	F6
Laird Weir	E4
Lambie Court	F7
Landsborough Court	F5
Landsborough Place	N5
Lauriston Court	E6
Lawson Drive	E3
Lennox Wynd	G4
Lesley Place	M6
Limekiln Road	M8
Lindsay Avenue	G6
Links Road	G5
Linn Road	D3
Linnburn Terrace	C3
Loanhead Road	E5
Loccard Road	K6
Lochlea Road	H4
Lochlie Place	M6
Lochranza Place	H5
Lochwood Gardens	G5
Longcraigs Avenue	D2
Longfield Avenue	F5
Longfield Place	F5
Lumsden Place	M6
Lundholm Road	M8
McDowall Avenue	E5
McDowall Place	D4
McGillivray Avenue	G5
McGregor Avenue	L6
McIsaac Road	H8
McKellar Avenue	E5
McKillop Place	G5
McKinnon Place	H5
McMillan Drive	B3
McNay Crescent	G6
Main Street	L6
Manor, The	D2
Manse Street	F7
Mariners View	C6
Martin Square	H4
Mary Love Place	J6
Maxwell Place	M5
Mayfield Crescent	K6
Mayfield Grove	K6
Mayfield Place	H7
Mayfield Road (Saltcoats)	H6
Mayfield Road (Stevenston)	K6
Mayville Street	K6
Meiklelaught Place	H4
Melbourne Road	F8
Melbourne Terrace	F8
Mid Dykes Road	F5
Middlepart Crescent	H6
Middlepart	K5
Mill Farm	E2
Millar Road	H7
Miller Place	C3
Millglen Lodges	D1
Millglen Place	E3
Millglen Road	E3
Millhill Road	L6
Misk Knowes	M9
Mitchell Place	F6
Moffat Wynd	G4
Montfode Court	D3
Montfode Drive	C3
Montgomerie Court (1)	D6
Montgomerie Crescent	F7

continued overleaf...

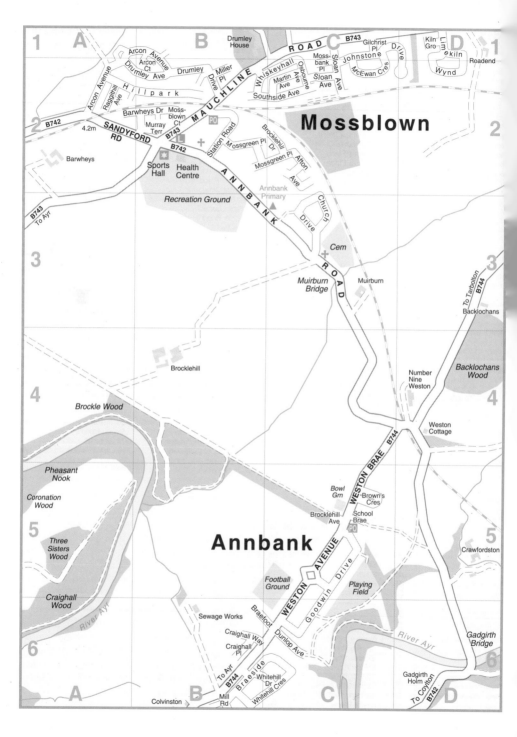

dex to Ardrossan

ntinued from page 9...

ontgomerie Pier Road	C5
ontgomerie Road	F7
ontgomerie Street	C6
oonlight Place	C5
oore Place	L7
oorpark Place	L8
oorpark Road East	L7
loorpark Road West	K8
Iorris Moodie Avenue	M8
Iorrison Avenue	M6
Iorrison Court	M6
lossgiel Place	M6
lossgiel Road (Ardrossan)	E3
lossgiel Road (Saltcoats)	H4
Motte Gardens	C3
Mount Pleasant	L6
Muir Drive	K7
Muir Drive Cottages	K7
Muirside Steadings	P5
Mulgrew Avenue	H5
Munnoch Crescent	C3
Munro Place	H5
Munro Walk	H5
Murdoch Court	F4
Murdoch Crescent	L8
Murray Avenue	F5
Nelson Road	J7
New England Road	H5
New Street	L7
Nineyard Street	G8
Nithsdale Road	E3
North Crescent Avenue	D4
North Crescent Road	C4
North Ring Road	P9
Nursery Place	E5
Oak Road	D3
Oakland Drive	M5
O'Connor Court	F7
Old Quarry Road	L7
Old Raise Road	H6
Owen Kelly Place	F6
Paisley Street	D5
Park Lane	D4
Park Road (Ardrossan)	D5
Park Road (Saltcoats)	F8
Park View	E4, E5
Park View Drive	E5
Parkend Avenue	H8
Parkend Gardens	H8
Parkend Road	H8
Parkhouse Gardens	E6
Parkhouse Road	E5
Patrick Avenue	K6
Pavilion Place	D6
Pinrmill Road	G5
Pladda Road	G5
Portland Place	L8
Primrose Place	H5
Princes Place	C6
Princes Street	C6
Prospecthill Road	H6
Quay Street	G8
Queen's Drive	D4
Raise Street	G6, G7
Rashley Square	E3
Raylight Place	C5
Red Gables Square	C4
Reid Terrace	H8
Reid's Avenue	L5
Rennie Place	G7
Riggs Cottages	K7
Roberston Crescent	H8
Rockpark Court	H8
Rosa Place	H5
Ross Road	G5
Rowanside Terrace	D3
St Andrews Court	G4
St Andrew's Place	N5
St Andrew's Road	E3
St Columba Place	N5
St Cuthbert's Court	F7
St James Place	N5
St John's Place (Ardrossan)	D5
St John's Place (Stevenston)	N5
St Lawrence Place	H6
St Margaret's Road	E3, E4
St Mary's Place	F6
St Medan's Place	G6
St Monach's Place	N5
St Ninian's Drive	E3
St Stephen's Place	N5
Saltcoats Road	J7
Salters Way	G4
Sanda Place	G5
Sandylands Promenade	H8
Sannox Drive	H5
Saughtree Avenue	G5
School Place	D5
Schoolwell Street	L6
Scott Place	F6
Seabank Street	H8
Seafield Court	C4
Seafield Drive	D4
Seaview Road	G8
Second Avenue	N8
Seton Lane	D5
Seton Street	D5
Sharphill Road	G7
Shaw Place	H5
Shellbridge Way	D5
Shore Road	L8
Sidney Street	F8
Simpson Drive	G4
Sinclair Street	K6
Skye Place	N5
Smith Drive	H7
Smithfield Terrace	L6
Solvents Road	Q10
Sommerville Drive	M9
Sorbie Road	E6, G2
South Beach Road	E6
South Beach Way	E6
South Crescent Road	D6
South Isle Road	D2
South Ring Road	P10
Spindrift Wynd	G4
Springvale Place	G7
Springvale Street	G7
Springwell Court	G7
Stanley Avenue	D4
Stanley Drive	D4
Stanley Place	F6
Stanley Road (Ardrossan)	D3
Stanley Road (Saltcoats)	F7
Station Road	L8
Stormlight Road	C6
Strathclyde Avenue	E4
Talisman Walk	H5
Taylor Place	G7
Thistle Terrace	M5
Thomas Campbell Street	H7
Three Sisters Court	F5
Tiree Place	N6
Town Square	L6
Townhead Road	H7
Townhead Street	L6
Trelawney Terrace	M9
Union Street	G8
Vernon Street	G8
Verona Place	E6
Victoria Place	G8
Victoria Road	G7
Wallace Avenue	L6
Warner Street	L8
Waverley Place	F6
Weavers Way	G4
Weir Road	E3
Wellpark Lane	G7
Wellpark Road	G7
Welsh Place	F6
West Road	P9
West Doura Avenue	G6
West Park Court	K7
Westfield Court	F8
Wheatley Gardens	H5
Wheatley Place	M6
Wheatley Road (Saltcoats)	H5
Wheatley Road (Stevenston)	M6
White Craig Road	E3
White Place	H4
Whitlees Court	F4
Whitlees Crescent	E4
Wilson Place	G4
Windmill Street	F8
Windmill Wynd	H4
Winton Buildings	C7
Winton Circus	F8
Winton Court	D6
Winton Lane	D5
Winton Place	D5
Winton Street (Ardrossan)	D5
Winton Street (Saltcoats)	F7
Witches Linn	C3
Woodland Place	D4
Wyllie Road	H7
Young Street	D5

Index to Annbank & Mossblown

Afton Avenue	C2
Annbank Road	B2
Arcon Avenue	B1
Arcon Court	B2
Barwheys Drive	A2
Braefoot	C6
Braeside	B6
Brocklehill Avenue	C5
Brocklehill Drive	C2
Brown's Crescent	C5
Church Drive	C3
Craighall Place	B6
Craighall Way	B6
Drumley Avenue	A2
Drumley Drive	B2
Dunlop Avenue	C6
Gadgirth Holm	D6
Gilchrist Place	C1
Goodwin Drive	C6
Hillpark	A2
Johnstone Drive	C1
Kiln Grove	D1
Limekiln Wynd	D1
McEwan Crescent	C2
Martin Avenue	C2
Mauchline Road	B2
Mill Road	B6
Miller Place	B2
Mossbank Place	C2
Mossblown Court	B2
Mossgreen Place	B2
Murray Terrace	B2
Osbourne Avenue	C2
Raggethill Avenue	A2
Sandyford Road	A2
School Brae	C5
Sloan Avenue	C1, C2
Southside Avenue	B2
Station Road	B2
Whiskeyhall	C2
Weston Avenue	C6
Weston Brae	C5
Whitehill Drive	C6
Whitehill Crescent	B6

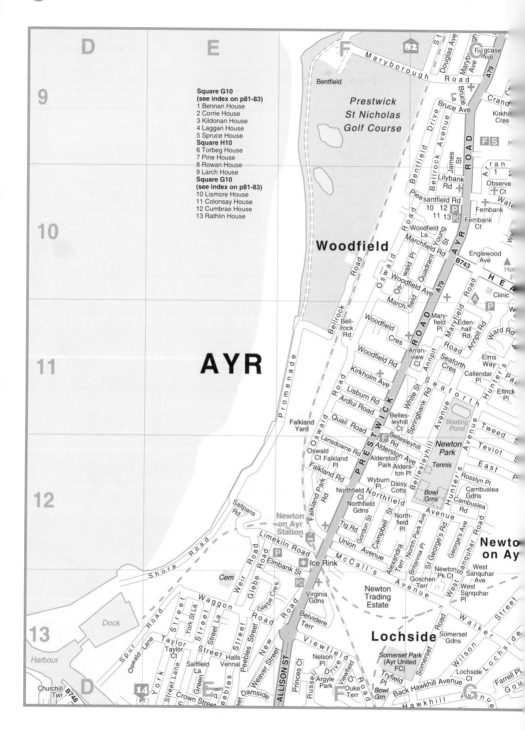

AYR

Woodfield

Prestwick
St Nicholas
Golf Course

Square G10
(see index on p81-83)
1 Bennan House
2 Corrie House
3 Kildonan House
4 Laggan House
5 Spruce House
Square H10
6 Torbeg House
7 Pine House
8 Rowan House
9 Larch House
Square G10
(see index on p81-83)
10 Lismore House
11 Colonsay House
12 Cumbrae House
13 Rathlin House

Newton
on Ay

Lochside

Dock

Harbour

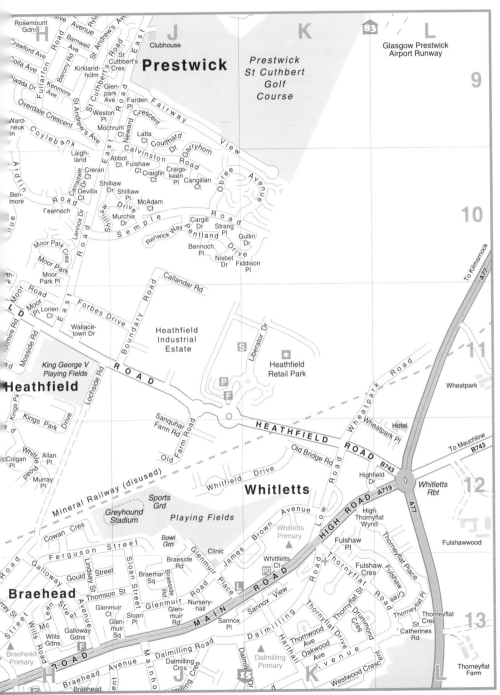

Index to street names in Prestwick can be found starting on page 81
Index to street names in Ayr can be found starting on page 94

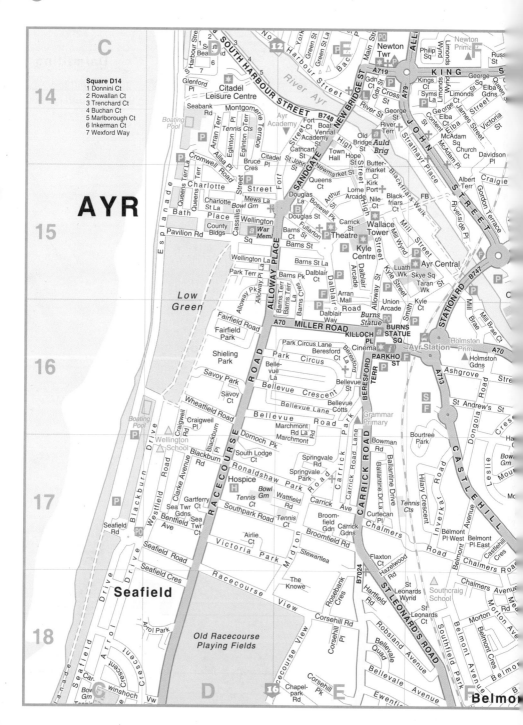

AYR

Square D14
1 Donnini Ct
2 Rowallan Ct
3 Trenchard Ct
4 Buchan Ct
5 Marlborough Ct
6 Inkerman Ct
7 Wexford Way

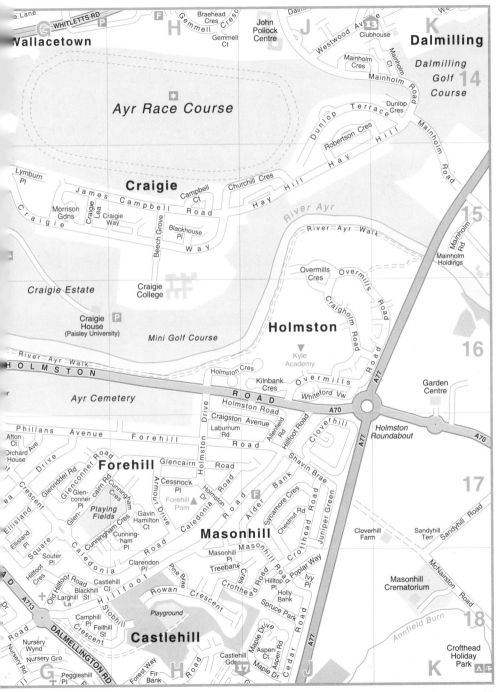

Wallacetown

WHITLETTS RD

Braehead Cres
Gemmell Cres
Gemmell Ct

John Pollock Centre

Westwood Ave

Clubhouse

Dalmilling

Mainholm Cres
Mainholm Ct

Mainholm Road

Dalmilling Golf Course

14

Ayr Race Course

Dunlop Terrace

Dunlop Cres

Robertson Cres

Mainholm Road

Lymburn Pl

Craigie

James Campbell Road

Campbell Ct
Churchill Cres

Hay Hill

Hay Hill

15

Craigie

Morrison Gdns
Craigie Lea
Craigie Way
Beech Grove
Blackhouse Pl
W a y

River Ayr

River Ayr Walk

Mainholm Rd

Mainholm Holdings

Craigie Estate

Craigie College

Overmills Cres
Overmills Road

Craigholm Road

Craigie House (Paisley University)

Mini Golf Course

Holmston

Kyle Academy

16

River Ayr Walk

HOLMSTON

Holmston Cres

Kilnbank Cres

Overmills Road

Whiteford Vw

Garden Centre

Ayr Cemetery

ROAD

Holmston Road

A70

Holmston Roundabout

A70

Phillans Avenue

Afton Ct
Orchard House

Forehill

Craigston Avenue
Laburnum Rd
Road

Allenfield Rd
Hilltop Road

Cloverhill

17

Forehill

Glencairn Road

Glenriddel Rd
Glenconner Road
Cairn Rd
Cunningham Cres
Cessnock Pl
Forehill Prim

Shavin Brae

Ellisland Crescent
Glenconner Pl
Glen-
Playing Fields
Gavin Hamilton Ct
Cunningham Cres

Alder Bank
Sycamore Cres
Chestnut Rd
Juniper Green

Cloverhill Farm

Sandyhill Terr
Sandyhill Road

Ellisland Pl
Square
Souter Pl
Cunningham Pl

Masonhill

Masonhill Pl
Masonhill Cres
Poplar Way
Ivy Pl

McNairston Road

Hilltop Cres
Old Hilltop Road
Clarendon Pl
Treebank

Hilltop Pl
Holly Bank

Masonhill Crematorium

Blackhill
Castlehill Ct
Larghill La
Stobhill St

Pine Brae
Rowan Crescent
Crofthead Road

Spruce Park

Annfield Burn

18

DALMELLINGTON RD

Camphill Crescent
Fellhill St

Playground

Castlehill

Maple Drive
Aspen Ct
Aspen Rd
Cedar Road

Crofthead Holiday Park

Nursery Wynd
Nursery Gro
Peggieshill Pl

Forest Way
Fir Bank

Castlehill Gdn

Maple Road

Index to street names can be found starting on page 94

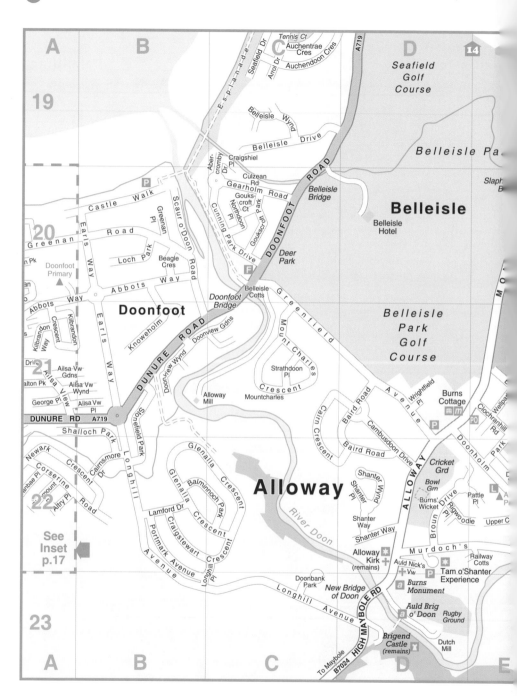

A B C D

19

A719

14

Tennis Ct
Auchentrae Cres
Auchendoon Cres

Seafield Golf Course

Seafield Dr

Arrol Dr

Esplanade

Belleisle Wynd

Belleisle Drive

Belleisle Pa...

Slaph...
B...

Abercromby Dr

Craigshiel Pl

Culzean Rd

Gearholm Road

Gouks-croft Ct

Goukscroft Park

Northton

Cunning Park Drive

DOONFOOT ROAD

Belleisle Bridge

Belleisle

Belleisle Hotel

Castle Walk

P

Greenan Pl

Greenan Road

Scaur o'Doon Road

Earls Way

Greenan Road

Greenan

...n Pk

Doonfoot Primary

Loch Park

Beagle Cres

Abbots Way

Deer Park

F

20

Abbots Way

Earls Way

Knoweholm

Doonfoot

Doonfoot Bridge

Doonview Gdns

Belleisle Cotts

Greenfield

Belleisle Park Golf Course

Mo...

Kilbrandon Crescent

Kilbrandon Way

Kilbrandon

DUNURE ROAD

Doonview Wynd

Mount Charles

Strathdoon Pl

Crescent

Mountcharles

Wrightfield Pl

Burns Cottage

m

Clochranhill Rd

Park

21

Dri...

Ailsa Vw Gdns

...alton Pk

Ailsa View

George Pl

Ailsa Vw Wynd

Ailsa Vw Pl

Sloan

Stonefield Park

Alloway Mill

Cairn Crescent

Baird Road

Cambusdoon Drive

Avenue

P

PO

DUNURE RD **A719**

Shalloch Park

Longhill

Cairnsmore Dr

Baird Road

Cricket Grd

Doonholm Drive

Pattle Pl

Newark Crescent

...nbae Cr

Corserine Road

...mount

Altry Pl

Glenalla Crescent

Glenalla Park

Balminnoch Park

Alloway

Shanter Pl

Shanter Wynd

Bowl Grn

Burns' Wicket

ALLOWAY

Broun Drive

Pigwoodie

L

A...
Pr...

Upper C...

22

Lamford Dr

Craigstewart Crescent

River Doon

Shanter Way

Shanter Way

Murdoch's

Railway Cotts

See Inset p.17

Portmark Avenue

Longhill

Avenue

Alloway Kirk (remains)

Auld Nick's Vw

Tam o'Shanter Experience

P

Doonbank Park

New Bridge of Doon

Burns Monument

a

HIGH MAYBOLE RD

23

Longhill Avenue

Auld Brig o'Doon

a

Rugby Ground

Brigend Castle (remains)

Dutch Mill

To Maybole   B7024

A B C D E

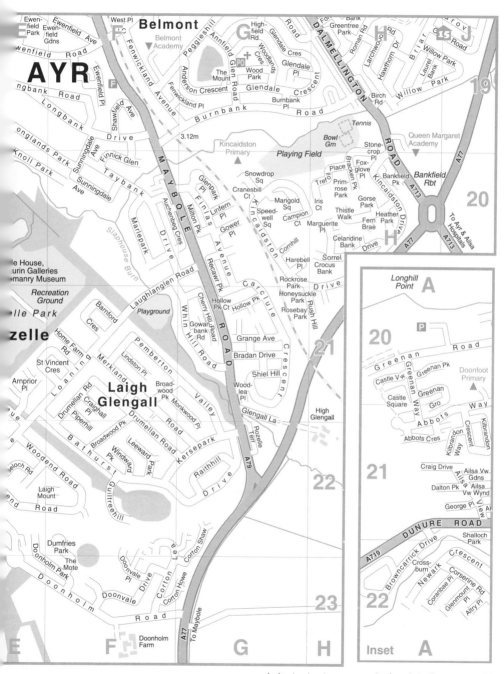

Index to street names can be found starting on page 94

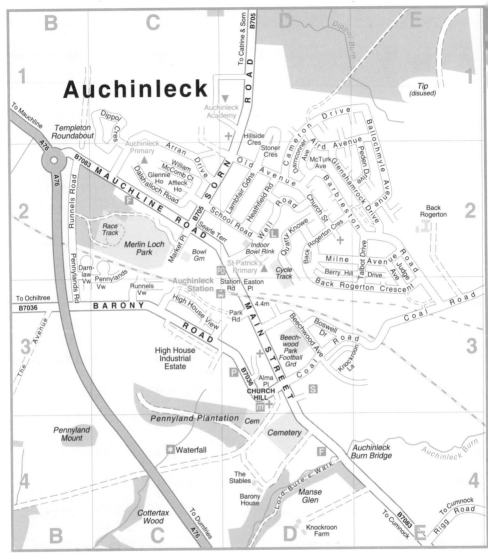

Index to Auchinleck

Affleck House	C2	Church Hill	D3	Judge Avenue	E2	Pennylands View	C2
Aird Avenue	D2	Church Street	D2	Knockroon Lane	D3	Quarry Knowe	D2
Alma Place	D3	Coal Road	D3	Lambfair Gardens	D2	Rigg Road	E4
Arran Drive	C2	Dalshalloch Road	D2	Lord Bute's Walk	D4	Runnels Road	B2
Avenue, The	B3	Darnconner Avenue	D2	McTurk Avenue	D2	Runnels View	C3
Back Rogerton Crescent	D2	Darnlaw View	B2	Main Street	D3	School Road	C2
Ballochmyle Avenue	E1	Dippol Crescent	C1	Market Place	C2	Searle Terrace	C2
Barbieston Road	D2	Easton Place	D3	Mauchline Road	D2	Sorn Road	C2
Barony Road	C3	Glennie House	C2	Milne Avenue	D2	Station Road	D3
Beechwood Avenue	D3	Glenshamrock Drive	D2	Old Avenue	D2	Stoner Crescent	D2
Berry Hill Drive	D2	Heathfield Road	D2	Park Road	D3	Talbot Drive	E2
Boswell Drive	D3	High House View	C3	Peden Drive	E2	Well Road	D2
Cameron Drive	D2	Hillside Crescent	D1	Pennylands Road	B2	William McComb Court	C2

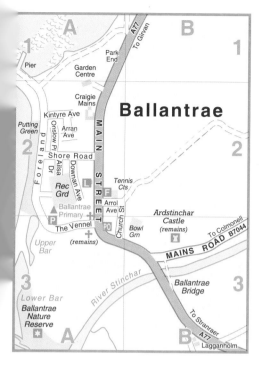

Index to Ballantrae

Ailsa Drive	A2
Arran Avenue	A2
Arrol Avenue	A2
Church Street	A3
Downan Avenue	A2
Foreland	A2
Kintyre Avenue	A2
Main Street	A2
Mains Road	B3
Onslow Place	A2
Park End	A1
Shore Road	A2
Vennel, The	A3

Index to Barrhill

Balluskie Cottages	B1
Gowlands Terrace	A2
Main Street	A2
Wallace Terrace	B2

Index to Barr

Avenue, The	B2
Changue Road	B2
Clachan, The	B2
Glebe Road	A2
Glenginnet Road	B2
Stincher Road	A2
Windy Row	B2

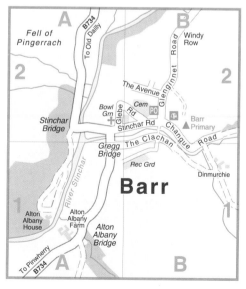

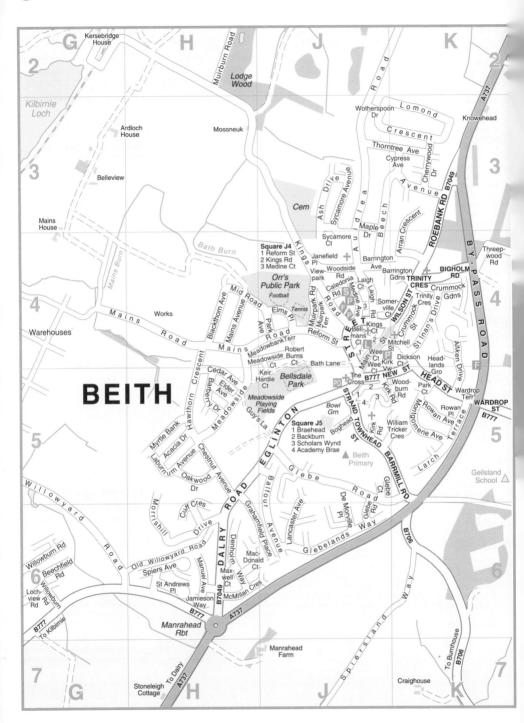

Index to Beith

Acacia Drive	H5
Academy Brae (4)	J5
Aitken Drive	K4
Arran Crescent	K4
Ash Drive	J3
Auldlea Road	J4
Backburn (2)	J5
Balfour Avenue	J6
Barberry Drive	H5
Barrington Avenue	J4
Barrington Gardens	K4
Barrmill Road	J5
Bath Lane	J4
Beech Avenue	J3
Beechfield Road	G6
Bellmans Close	J4
Bigholm Road	K4
Blackthorn Avenue	H4
Boghead	J5
Braehead (1)	J5
By-Pass Road	K4
Caledonia Road	J4
Cedar Avenue	H5
Cherrywood Drive	K3
Chestnut Avenue	H5
Cross, The	J5
Crummock Gardens	K4
Crummock Street	K4
Cuff Crescent	H6
Cypress Avenue	K3
Dalry Road	H6
De Morville Place	J6
Denholm Way	H6
Dickson Court	K4
Eglinton Street	J5
Elder Avenue	H5
Elms Place	J4
Glebe Court	J5
Glebe Road	J5, J6
Glebelands Way	J6
Grahamfield Place	H6
Guy's Lane	J5
Hawthorn Crescent	H5
Head Street	K5
Headlands Grove	K4
Jamieson Way	H6
Janefield Place	J4
Keir Hardie Court	J5
Kings Court	J4
Kings Road (2)	J4
Kirk Road	J5
Kirk View	J5
Laburnum Avenue	H5
Laigh Court	J4
Laigh Road	J4
Lancaster Avenue	J6
Larch Terrace	K5
Lochview Road	G6
Lomond Crescent	K3
MacDonald Court	H6
McMillan Crescent	H6
Main Street	J4
Mains Avenue	H4
Mains Road	H4
Manuel Avenue	H6
Maple Drive	J3
Maxwell Court	H6
Meadowbank Terrace	J4
Meadowside Court	H4
Meadowside	H5

Medine Avenue	J4
Medine Court (3)	J4
Mid Road	H4
Mitchell Street	K4
Montgomerie Avenue	K5
Morrishill Drive	H6
Muirburn Road	H2
Muirpark Road	J4
Muirpark Terrace	J4
Myrtle Bank	H5
New Street	J5
Oakwood Drive	H5
Old Willowyard Road	H6
Park Avenue	J4
Park Court	K5
Reform Street (1)	J4
Robert Burns Court	J4
Roebank Road	K4
Rowan Avenue	K5
Rowan Place	K5
St Andrews Place	H6
St Inan's Drive	K4
Scholars Wynd (3)	J5

Somerville Court	J4
Spiers Avenue	H6
Spiersland Way	J7
Strand	J5
Sycamore Avenue	J3
Sycamore Court	J4
Thorntree Avenue	J3
Threepwood Road	K4
Townhead Street	J5
Trinity Crescent	K4
Viewpark	J4
Wardrop Street	K5
Wardrop Terrace	K5
Wee Close	J4
Wee Court	J4
William Tricker Crescent	K5
Willowburn Road	G6
Willowyard Road	G5
Wilson Street	K4
Woodburn Road	K5
Woodside Road	J4
Wotherspoon Drive	J3

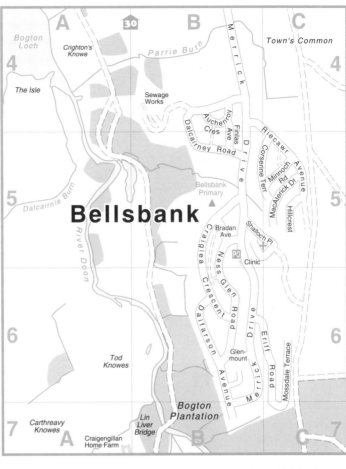

Index to Bellsbank

Auchenroy Crescent	B4
Bradan Avenue	B5
Corserine Terrace	C5
Craiglea Crescent	B5
Dalcairney Road	B4
Dalfarson Avenue	B6
Eriff Road	C6
Finlas Avenue	B4
Glenmount	B6
Hillcrest	C5
MacAterick Drive	C5
Merrick Drive	B4, B6
Minnoch Road	C5
Mossdale Terrace	C6
Ness Glen Road	B5
Riecawr Avenue	C4
Shalloch Place	B5

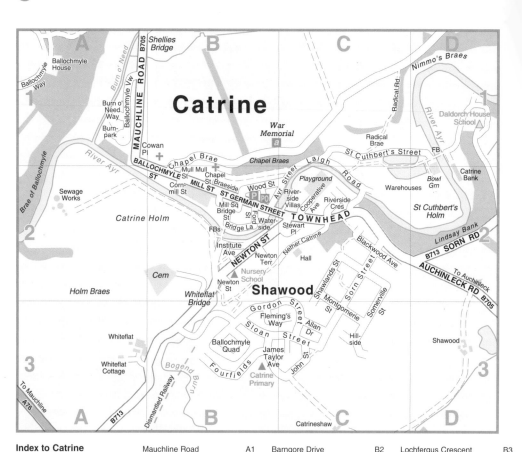

Index to Catrine

Allan Drive	C3
Auchinleck Road	D2
Ayr Street	B2
Ballochmyle House	A1
Ballochmyle Quadrant	B3
Ballochmyle Street	B2
Ballochmyle View	A1
Ballochmyle Way	A1
Blackwood Avenue	C2
Braeside	B2
Bridge Lane	B2
Bridge Street	B2
Burn o' Need Way	A1
Burnpark	A1
Chapel Brae	B1
Chapel Street	B2
Cooperative Avenue	C2
Cornmill Street	B2
Cowan Place	B1
Fleming's Way	B3
Ford Street	B2
Fourfields	B3
Gordon Street	B3
Hillside	C3
Institute Avenue	B2
James Taylor Avenue	B3
John Street	C3
Laigh Road	C1

Mauchline Road	A1
Mill Square	B2
Mill Street	B2
Montgomerie Street	C3
Mull Mull Street	B2
Nether Catrine	C2
Newton Street	B2
Newton Terrace	B2
Radical Brae	C1
Radical Road	C1
Riverside Crescent	C2
Riverside Villas	C2
St Cuthbert's Street	C1
St Germain Street	B2
Shawlands Street	C2
Sloan Street	B3
Somerville Street	C3
Sorn Road	D2
Sorn Street	C2
Stewart Place	C2
Townhead	C2
Waterside	B2
Wood Street	B2

Index to Coyton

Arthurston Terrace	B2
Ashgrove	B2
Barclaugh Drive	A2

Barngore Drive	B2
Beeches, The	B2
Broadwood	B2
Bryden Place	C3
Burgoyne Drive	B2
Carnell Drive	B2
Carrick View	B1
Chestnut Grove	B2
Coats Place	B3
Dalblair Crescent	B2
Dalrymple View	B3
Douglas Brown Place	B3
Douglas Road	B2
Drumcoyle Drive	B1
Drumsuy Court	B3
Fergus Way	B2
Gadgirth Court	B2
Gallowhill Farm	C2
Gallowhill Quadrant	B1
Garvine Road	B2
Glenhead Court	C2
Glenhead Place	C3
Hamilton Place	B3
Highpark Road	C3
Hole Road	B2
John Hodge Court	B2
Kyle Crescent	B1
Laighpark Court	A2
Laighpark Road	A2
Laighpark View	A2

Lochfergus Crescent	B3
Lochfergus Drive	B3
Lochfergus Place	B3
Lochfergus Wynd	B3
Martnaham Drive	B2
Meadow Park	B2
Milton Park	B2
Murray Park	B2
Park Terrace	B2
Parklands	B2
Potterhill Place	B3
Ramseyston Drive	B2
St Brides Way	C3
Shaw Place	C3
Springs Park	C3
Sundrum Park	B1
Thorn Avenue	B2
Whitehill Way	B2
Woodhead Road	B1

Index to Colmonell

Craigneil Road	B2
Haddow Place	B2
Hyslop Crescent	B2
Kirkhill Crescent	B1
Main Street	B2
Manse Road	A2
Rowantree Street	A2

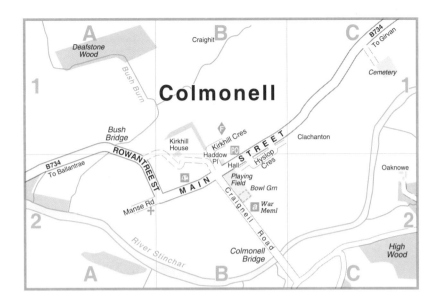

Colmonell

Deafstone Wood
Craighit
B734 To Girvan
Cemetery
Bush Burn
Bush Bridge
Kirkhill Cres
Kirkhill House
Clachanton
ROWANTREE ST
B734 To Ballantrae
Haddow Pl
PO
Hall
Hyslop Cres
STREET
MAIN
Oaknowe
Manse Rd
Playing Field
Bowl Grn
Craignell Road
War Meml
River Stinchar
Colmonell Bridge
High Wood

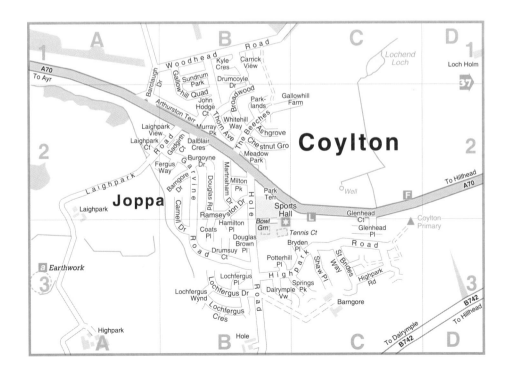

Coylton

Joppa

Woodhead Road
A70 To Ayr
Barclaugh Dr
Gallowhill Quad
Sundrum Park
Kyle Cres
Carrick View
Drumcoyle Dr
Broadwood
Lochend Loch
Loch Holm
B7
Arthurston Terr
John Hodge Ct
Thorn Ave
Park-lands
Gallowhill Farm
Laighpark View
Murray Pk
Whitehill Way
The Beeches
Ashgrove
Laighpark Ct
Road
Gadgirth Ct
Dalblair Cres
The Chestnut Gro
Burgoyne Dr
Meadow Park
To Hillhead A70
Laighpark
Fergus Way
Garvine Road
Douglas Rd
Marnham Dr
Milton Pk
Park Terr
Well
F
Laighpark
Barngore Dr
Carnell Dr
Ramseyston Dr
Hole
Sports Hall
Glenhead Ct
L
Glenhead Pl
Coylton Primary
a Earthwork
Hamilton Pl
Coats Pl
Bowl Grn
Tennis Ct
Road
Drumsuy Ct
Douglas Brown Pl
Bryden Pl
Potterhill Pl
Highpark
Shaw Pl
St Brides Way
Highpark Rd
Lochfergus Pl
Highpark
Springs Pk
Lochfergus Dr
Dalrymple Vw
Barngore
Lochfergus Wynd
Road
Lochfergus Cres
B742 To Hillhead
Highpark
Hole
To Dalrymple B742

Index to Crookedholm

Cowans Row	A2
Grougar Road	A1
Leaveret Lea	B1
Main Road	A2
Meadowside	B1
Milton Road	A1
Ralston Drive	A1
Ralstonyards Road	B2
Reid Court	B2
Seright Crescent	A2
Seright Square	A1
Silverwood Road	A1
Struthers Avenue	A1
Wellington Avenue	A1
Wellington Gardens	B1

Index to Crosshill

Back Street	C2
Bruce Square	C2
Carrick Drive	C2
Dailly Road	B3
Dalduff Cottages	A2
Dalhowan Street	C3
King Street	B1

Kirkbride Crescent
Kirkmichael Road
Milton Street
Newton Street

Index to Crosshous Knockentiber

Annandale Court
Annandale Crescent
Annandale Gardens
Annandale Lane
Annandale View
Barr Avenue
Busbie Cottages
Busbie Gardens
Busbie View
Carmel Place
Castle Terrace
Corse Place
Craig Drive
Craigie Place
Craiglea Avenue
Craufurdhill Place
Credon Drive
Crossdene Road
Index continued below...

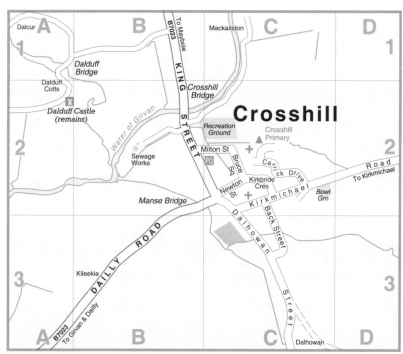

Index continued from above...

		Hannah Drive	C2	Loudoun Place	C5	Springfield Road	C3
		Hemphill View	C2	Mote View	A4	Springhill Avenue	B5
Dean Place	C5	Hunter Road	C4	Parkhill Avenue	B5	Thornton Avenue	B4
Fisher Court	C2	Irvine Road	B4	Plann Cottages	C2	Windyedge Cottages	C5
Fisher Way	A4	Kilmarnock Road	B4	Plann Road	C1	Woodbank Road	C4
Fardalehill View	C4	Kilmaurs Road	B3	Playingfield Crescent	B4	Woodlea Court	C3
Gatehead Road	B4	Laigh Milton Road	B4	Playingfield Road	B4	Woodlea Crescent	C3
Greenhill Terrace	C2	Laurieland Avenue	B4	Southhook Road	B2	Wyndford Cottages	C1

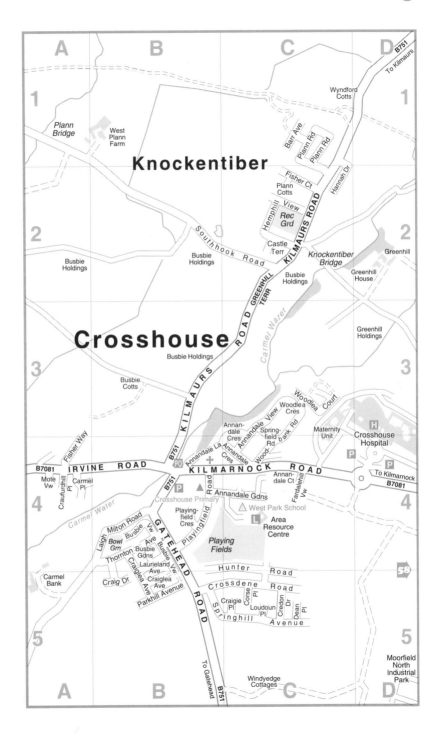

Knockentiber

Crosshouse

A B C D

B751
To Kilmaurs

1

Wyndford Cotts

Plann Bridge
West Plann Farm

Bar Ave
Plann Rd
Plann Rd

Hannah Dr

Fisher Ct

Plann Cotts

View
Hemphill
KILMAURS ROAD

Rec Grd

2

Southhook Road

Castle Terr

Knockentiber Bridge

Greenhill

Busbie Holdings
Busbie Holdings
Busbie Holdings

Greenhill House

KILMAURS ROAD
GREENHILL TERR

Carmel Water

Greenhill Holdings

Busbie Holdings

3

Busbie Cotts

Fisher Way

Woodlea Court
Woodlea Cres
Woodlea View
Annandale View
Annandale Cres
Springfield Rd
Woodbank Rd
Wood...

Maternity Unit

H
Crosshouse Hospital

B7081
IRVINE ROAD

Annandale La
Annandale Cres

KILMARNOCK ROAD

P
To Kilmarnock
B7081

PO

Mote Vw
Craufurdhill Pl
Carmel Pl

P

Annandale Ct
Fardalehill Vw

Crosshouse Primary

Annandale Gdns

West Park School

4

Carmel Water

Milton Road
Laigh Busbie Vw
Bowl Grn
Thornton
Busbie Ave
Busbie Gdns
Busbie Vw
Laurieland Ave
Craiglea Ave
Craig Dr
Craiglea Ave
Parkhill Avenue

Playingfield Cres
Playingfield Road

GATEHEAD ROAD

Playing Fields

L
Area Resource Centre

Hunter Road

58

Carmel Bank

Crossdene Road

Craigie Pl
Corse Pl
Loudoun Pl
Credon Dr
Dean Pl

Springhill Avenue

5

Moorfield North Industrial Park

To Gatehead

B751

Windyedge Cottages

A B C D

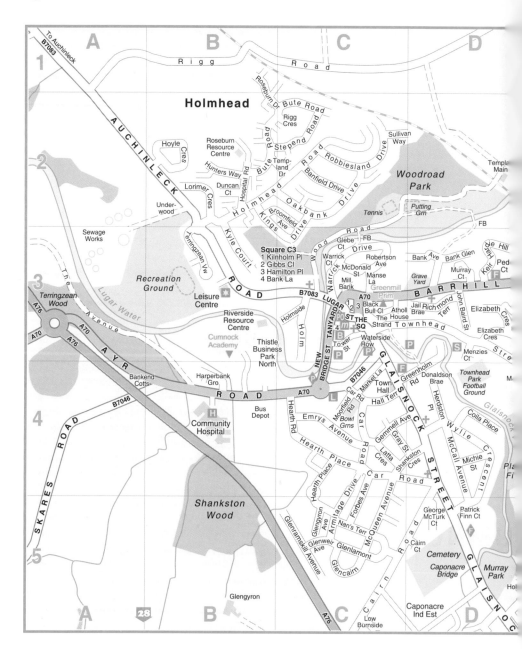

Holmhead

Square C3
1 Kilnholm Pl
2 Gibbs Cl
3 Hamilton Pl
4 Bank La

Woodroad Park

Recreation Ground

Leisure Centre

Riverside Resource Centre

Cumnock Academy

Thistle Business Park North

Harperbank Gro

Community Hospital

Bus Depot

Shankston Wood

Glengyron

Terringzean Wood

Sewage Works

Hoyle Cres

Roseburn Resource Centre

Hunters Way

Lorimer Cres

Duncan Ct

Underwood

Rigg Cres

Bute Road

Stepend Road

Robbiesland Drive

Sullivan Way

Templand Main

Banfield Drive

Oakbank Drive

Kings Drive

Broomfield Ave

Tennis

Putting Grn

Glebe

Warrick Ct

McDonald St

Robertson Ave

Manse La

Mill Bank

Bank Ave

Bank Glen

Murray Ct

Grave Yard

Greenmill Prim

Black

Bull Cl

Atholl House

The Strand

Jail Brae

Richmond Terr

John Baird St

Elizabeth Cres

Elizabeth Cres

Townhead

Waterside Row

Menzies Ct

Tower

Holm

Holmside

Town Hall

Hall Terr

Market La

Greenholm Rd

Donaldson Brae

Townhead Park Football Ground

Herdston Pl

Coila Place

Emrys Avenue

Moorfield Rd

Gemmell Ave

Gray St

Latta Cres

Shankston Cres

Wylie Crescent

McCall Avenue

Michie St

Bankend Cotts

Hearth Rd

Hearth Place

Bowl Grns

Glengyron Ave

Armitage Drive

Forbes Ave

Nan's Terr

McQueen Avenue

Glenweir Ave

Glenlamont

Glencairn

George McTurk Ct

Patrick Finn Ct

Cairn Ct

Cemetery

Caponacre Bridge

Murray Park

Caponacre Ind Est

Low Burnside

Glentamskill Avenue

To Auchinleck

B7083

Rigg Road

Roseburn Dr

Hospital Rd

Bute Road

Templand Dr

Holmhead Road

Wood Drive

Kyle Court

Terringzean Vw

Lugar Water

The

A76

A70

A76

A70

A76

Ayr Avenue

Skares Road

B7046

Road

A70

B7046

Road

New Bridge St

Tanyard

Lugar

B7083

Warrick

St The Sq

Post

Glaisnock Street

Cairn Road

A76

Barrhill

FB

FB

FB

P

P

P

P

P

P

S

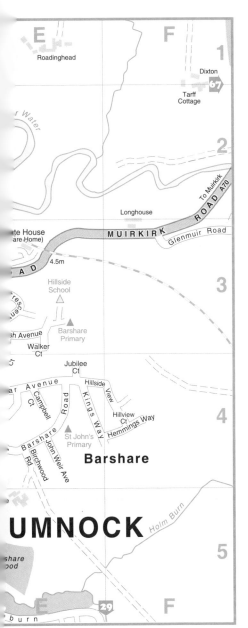

Index to Cumnock

Armitage Drive	C5	Hearth Road	C4
Atholl Hosue	C3	Hemmings Way	F4
Auchinleck Road	A2	Herdston Place	D4
Avenue, The	A3	Hillside View	E4
Avisyard Avenue	F6	Hillview Court	F4
Ayr Road	A3	Holland Crescent	E3
Ballantyne Court	E3	Holm	C3
Banfield Drive	C2	Holmburn Avenue	E5
Bank Avenue	D3	Holmburn Close	D5
Bank Glen	D3	Holmburn Place	E6
Bank Lane (4)	C3	Holmburn Road	E5
Bankend Cottages	A4	Holmhead Road	B2
Barrhill Road	D3	Holmside	C3
Barrhill Terrace	E3	Hospital Road	B2
Barshare Road	E4	Hoyle Crescent	B2
Birchwood Road	E4	Hunter's Way	B2
Black Bull Close	C3	Jail Brae	D3
Blackfaulds Road	E6	James Young Avenue	E6
Broomfield Avenue	C2	John Allan Drive	D6
Buntens Close	E7	John Baird Street	D3
Bute Road	B2, C2	John Weir Avenue	E4
Cairn Court	D5	Jubilee Court	E4
Cairn Road	C6	Keir Hardie Hill	D3
Cairnscadden Road	F6	Kilbrennan Avenue	F7
Cameron Crescent	D6	Kings Drive	B2
Campbell Court	E4	Kings Way	E4
Car Road	C4	Kilnholm Place (1)	C3
Carsgailloch Avenue	E6	Kyle Court	B3
Church Court	E6	Lamont Crescent	E6
Coila Place	D4	Latta Crescent	C4
Craigens Place	E6	Link Road	D3
Craigens Road	E6	Lorimer Crescent	B2
Dalgleish Avenue	E3	Low Burnside	C5
Davaar Avenue	F6	Lugar Street	C3
Donaldson Brae	D4	McCall Avenue	D4
Drumbrochan Road	D3	McClymont Court	E4
Duncan Court	B2	McDonald Street	C3
Edgar Avenue	E4	McIntyre Crescent	F6
Elizabeth Crescent	D3	McQueen Avenue	C5
Emrys Avenue	C4	McTurk Road	E6
Forbes Avenue	C5	Manse Lane	C3
Gemmell Avenue	C4	Market Lane	C4
George McTurk Court	D5	Meagher Court	D4
Gibbs Close (2)	C3	Menzies Avenue	E6
Glaisnock Glen	E7	Menzies Court	D3
Glaisnock Road	D5, E7	Michie Street	D4
Glaisnock Street	C3, D5	Mill Bank	C3
Glaisnock View	E6	Moorfield Road	C4
Glebe Court	C3	Muirkirk Road	F3
Glencairn	C5	Murray Court	D3
Glengyron Avenue	C5	Nans Terrace	C5
Glenlamont	C5	Netherthird Place	E6
Glenmuir Road	F3	Netherthird Road	E6
Glenramskill Avenue	C5	New Bridge Street	C4
Glenweir Avenue	C5	Oakbank Drive	C2
Gray Street	C4	Patrick Finn Court	D5
Greenholm Road	D4	Peden Court	D3
Hall Terrace	C4	Penders Wynd	E7
Hamilton Place (3)	C3	Phillips Wynd	E7
Harperbank Grove	B4	Richmond Terrace	D3
Hearth Place	C4	Rigg Crescent	C2
		Robbiesland Drive	C2
		continued overleaf...	

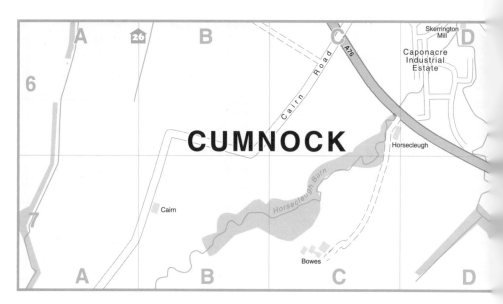

Index to Dailly

Back Road	B2	Hazelwood Avenue	C2
Bridge Street	B1	Linfern Road	C1
Brunston Avenue	A1	Loaning, The	C2
Brunston Wynd	A2	Main Street	B2, C1
Church Crescent	B2	Smith Crescent	B2
Eldinton Terrace	B2	Victory Crescent	C1
Golf Course Road	A2	West End	B2
Greenhead Street	C1	Wood Street	B2
Hadyard Terrace	C2	Woodside	B2

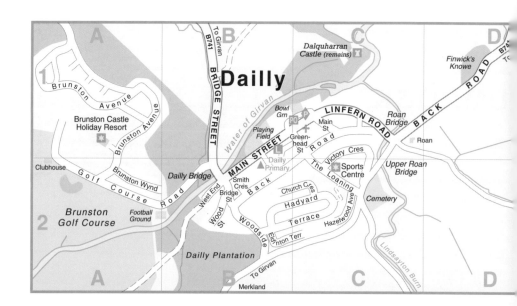

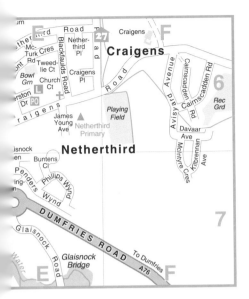

Craigens

Netherthird

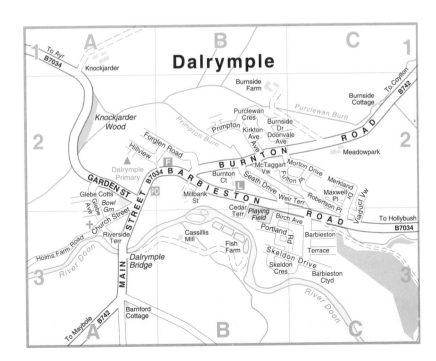

Dalrymple

Index to Cumnock
continued from page 27...

Rigg Road	B1
River View	E4
Robertson Avenue	C3
Roseburn Drive	B1
Ryderston Drive	E6
Shankston Crescent	E4
Skares Road	A4
Skerrington	E7
Skerrington Place	D5
Square, The	C3
Stepend Road	C2
Strand, The	C3
Sullivan Way	C2
Tanyard	C3
Templand Drive	C2
Terringzean View	B3
Tower Street	C3
Townhead Street	D3
Tweedlie Court	E6
Underwood	B2
Walker Court	E3
Warrick Court	C3
Warrick Drive	C3
Waterside Row	C3
Wood Road	C3
Wylie Crescent	D4

Index to Dalrymple

Barbieston Courtyard	C3
Barbieston Road	B2
Barbieston Terrace	C3
Birch Avenue	C3
Burnside Drive	B2
Burnton Court	B2
Burnton Road	B2
Cedar Terrace	B3
Church Street	A3
Doonvale Avenue	B2
Forglen Road	A2
Fulton Place	B2
Garden Street	A2
Glebe Avenue	A2
Glebe Cottages	A2
Hillview	A2
Holms Farm Road	A3
Kirkton Avenue	B2
McTaggart View	B2
Main Street	A3
Maxwell Place	C2
Merkland Drive	C3
Millbank Street	B2
Morton Drive	C2
Portland Road	B3
Primpton Avenue	B2
Purclewan Crescent	B2
Riverside Terrace	A3
Robertson Place	C2
Seath Drive	B2
Skeldon Crescent	B3
Skeldon Drive	B3
Viaduct View	C3
Weir Terrace	B2

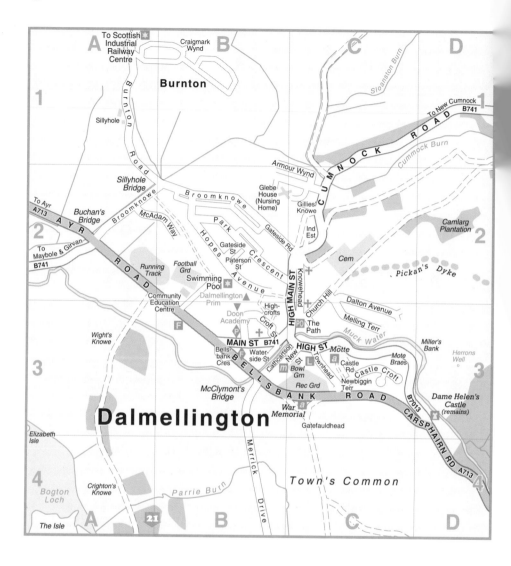

Index to Dalmellington

Armour Wynd	B2	Croft Street	B3	Main Street		B3
Ayr Road	A2	Cumnock Road	C1	McAdam Way		A2
Bellsbank Crescent	B3	Dalton Avenue	C2	Melling Terrace		C3
Bellsbank Road	B3	Gatefauldhead	C3	Merrick Drive		B4
Broomknowe	A2, B2	Gateside Road	B2	New Street		C3
Burnton Road	A1	Gateside Street	B2	Newbiggin Terrace		C3
Carsphairn Road	D4	Gillies' Knowe	C2	Park Crescent		B2
Castle Croft	C3	High Main Street	C3	Paterson Street		B2
Castle Road	C3	High Street	C3	Path, The		C3
Cathcartson	B3	Highcrofts	B3	Townhead		C3
Church Hill	C3	Hopes Avenue	B2	Waterside Street		B3
Craigmark Wynd	B1	Knowehead	C2			

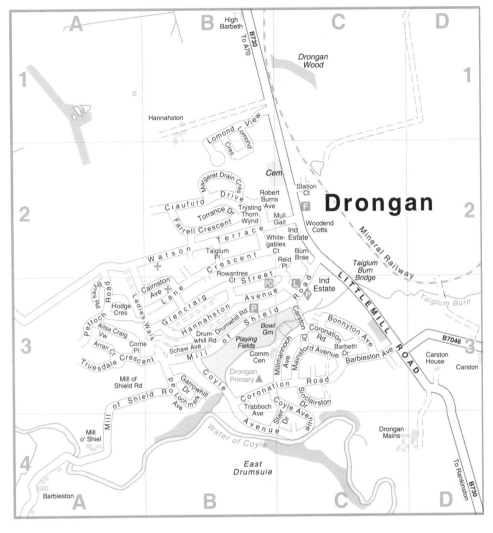

Drongan

Index to Drongan

Ailsa Craig View	A3	Farrell Crescent	B2
Arran Court	A3	Garrowhill Drive	B3
Barbeth Drive	C3	Glencraig Street	B3
Barbieston Avenue	C3	Hannahston Avenue	B3
Bonnyton Avenue	C3	Hodge Crescent	A3
Burn Brae	C2	Lane Crescent	B3
Byres Road	A3	Ladies Walk	A3
Cairnston Avenue	B3	Littlemill Road	C3
Carston Drive	C3	Lochmark Avenue	B3
Coronation Road	B3, C3	Lomond Crescent	B1
Corrie Place	A3	Lomond View	B1
Coyle Avenue	B3	Mainsford Avenue	C3
Craufurd Drive	B2	Margaret Drain Crescent	B2
Drumwhill Road	B3	Millmannoch Avenue	C3
		Mill of Shield Road	A4, B3
		Mull Gait	C2

Pettoch Road	A3
Reid Place	C2
Robert Burns Avenue	B2
Rowantree Court	B2
Schaw Avenue	B3
Sinclairston Drive	C3
Stair Drive	C4
Station Court	C2
Taiglum Place	B2
Torrance Drive	B2
Trabboch Avenue	B3
Truesdale Crescent	A3
Trysting Thorn Wynd	B2
Watson Terrace	B2
Whitegables Court	B2
Woodend Cottages	C2

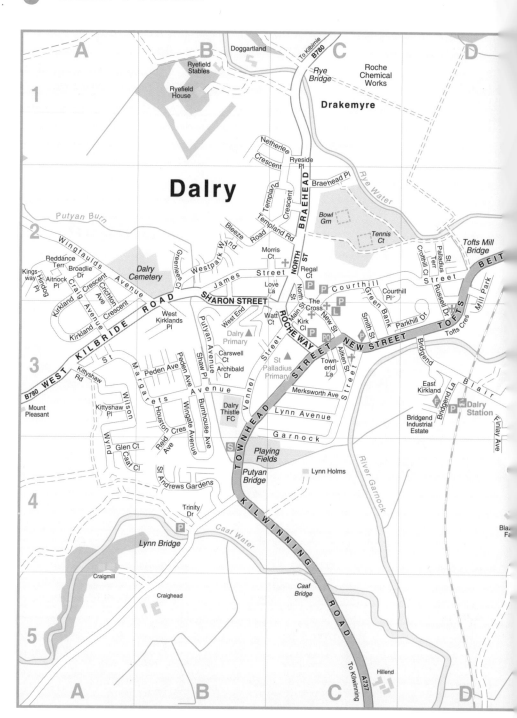

Dalry

Doggartland

To Kilbirnie B780

Rye Bridge

Roche Chemical Works

Drakemyre

Ryefield Stables

Ryefield House

Netherlee Crescent

Ryeside Pl

Braehead Pl

Rye Water

Templand Crescent

BRAEHEAD ST

Bleeze Road

Templand Rd

Bowl Grn

Tennis Ct

Putyan Burn

Wingfauld's Avenue

Greenlees Ct

Westpark Wynd

Dalry Cemetery

Morris Ct

NORTH ST

Regal Ct

St Palladius Terr

Crothill Ct

Russell Dr

Mill Park

Tofts Mill Bridge

BEIT

Reddance Terr

Broadlie Dr

Aitnock Pl

Crichton Ave

Crescent

James Street

Street

Courthill

Green Bank

Courthill Pl

Street

Kings-way

Hindog Pl

Kirkland Crescent

Crichton Ave

Crescent

SHARON STREET

Love La

N St

The Cross

Smith St

Parkhill Dr

TOFTS

Tofts Cres

Kirkland

West Kirklands Pl

West End

Watt Ct

Main St

Kirk Cl

New St

Green Bank

KILBRIDE ROAD

Putyan Avenue

Dalry Primary

St Palladius Primary

New Street

Aitken Street

NEW STREET

Bridgend

St

Kittyshaw Rd

Margarets

Peden Ave

Shaw Pl

Carswell Ct

Archibald Dr

ROCHE WAY

Town-end La

Merksworth Ave

East Kirkland

B780 WEST

Kittyshaw Pl

Wilson

Houston Cres

Peden Ave

Wingate Avenue

Avenue

Burnhouse Ave

Vennel Street

TOWNHEAD STREET

Lynn Avenue

Bridgend La

Dalry Station

Mount Pleasant

Wynd

Reid Ave

Dalry Thistle FC

Garnock

Bridgend Industrial Estate

Finlay Ave

Blair

Glen Ct

Caaf Cl

St Andrews Gardens

Playing Fields

Putyan Bridge

Lynn Holms

River Garnock

Trinity Dr

Lynn Bridge

Caaf Water

KILWINNING ROAD

Craigmill

Craighead

Caaf Bridge

Bla Fa

To Kilwinning

A737

Hillend

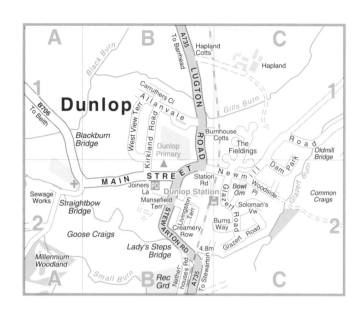

Index to Dalry

Aitken Street	C3	Kirkland Crescent	A3	Watt Court	C3
Aitnock Place	A2	Kittyshaw Place	A3	West End	B3
Archibald Drive	B3	Kittyshaw Road	A3	West Kilbride Road	A3
Beith Road	D2	Love Lane	C2	West Kirklands Place	B3
Blair Road	D3	Lynn Avenue	C3	Westpark Wynd	B2
Blairlands Drive	E3	Main Street	C3	Wilson Wynd	A3
Bleeze Road	B2	Mair Avenue	E3	Wingate Avenue	B3
Braehead Place	C2	Merksworth Avenue	C3	Wingfaulds Avenue	A2
Braehead	C2	Mill Park	D3		
Braidland Avenue	E4	Morris Court	B2		
Bridgend Lane	D3	Netherlee Crescent	B1		
Bridgend	D3	New Street	C3		
Broadlie Drive	A2	North Street	C2		
Burnhouse Avenue	B3	Parkhill Drive	D3	**Index to Dunlop**	
Caaf Close	A4	Peden Avenue	B3		
Carswell Court	B3	Putyan Avenue	B3	Allanvale	B1
Cleeves Avenue	E4	Reddance Terrace	A2	Burnhouse Cottages	B1
Courthill Place	C2	Regal Court	C2	Burns Way	C2
Courthill Street	C2	Reid Avenue	B4	Carruthers Close	B1
Craig Avenue	A2	Roche Way	C3	Creamery Row	B2
Crichton Avenue	A2	Russell Drive	D2	Dam Park	C2
Crofthill Close	D2	Ryeside Place	C1	Fieldings, The	C1
Cross, The	C3	St Andrews Gardens	B4	Glazert Road	C2
Douglas Avenue	D3	St Margarets Avenue	A3	Hapland Cottages	B1
East Kirkland	D3	St Palladius Terrace	D2	Joiners Lane	B2
Finlay Avenue	D3	Sharon Street	B2	Kirkland Road	B1
Garnock Street	C3	Shaw Place	B3	Livingston Terrace	B2
Glen Court	A4	Smith Street	C3	Lugton Road	B1
Green Bank	C2	Stoopshill Crescent	D3	Main Street	B2
Greenlees Court	B2	Templand Crescent	B2	Mansefield Terrace	B2
Hindog Place	A2	Templand Road	B2	Netherhouses Road	B2
Houston Crescent	B3	Tofts Crescent	B3	Newmill Road	C2
James Street	B2	Tofts	B3	Soloman's View	C2
Kerse Avenue	E3	Townend Lane	C3	Station Road	B2
Kilwinning Road	B4	Townhead Street	B4	Stewarton Road	B2
Kingsway	A2	Trinity Drive	B4	West View Terrace	B1
Kirk Close	C3	Vennel Street	B3	Woodside Place	C2

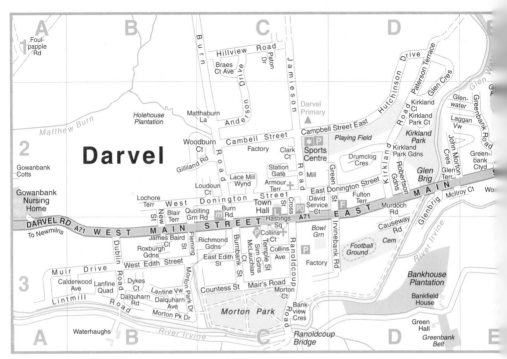

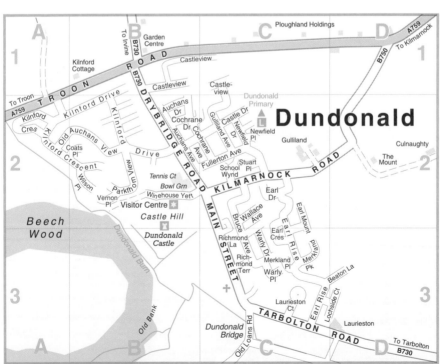

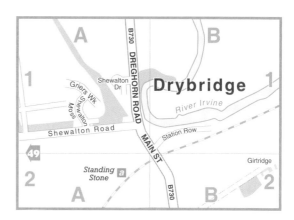

Drybridge

Index to Darvel

Anderson Drive	C2
Armour Terrace	C2
Bankview Crescent	C3
Blair Terrace	B2
Braes Court Avenue	C1
Burn Road	C1, C2
Burnbank Street	C3
Calderwood Avenue	B3
Campbell Street East	C2
Campbell Street	C2
Causeway Road	D3
Clark Court	C2
Collins Avenue	C3
Collins Court	C3
Countess Street	C3
Cross Street	C2
Dalquharn Avenue	B3
Dalquharn Road	B3
Darvel Road	A3
David Service Court	C2
Drumclog Crescent	D2
Dublin Road	B3
Dykes Court	B3
East Donington Street	D2
East Edith Street	C3
East Main Street	D2
Fleming Street	B3
Foulpapple Road	A2
Fulton Terrace	D2
George Young Drive	E2
Gilliland Road	B2
Glen Crescent	D2
Glen Terrace	D2
Glenbrig	D2
Glenwater	E2
Gowanbank Cottages	A2
Green Street	D2
Greenbank Courtyard	E2
Greenbank Road	E2
Hastings Square	C3
Hillview Road	C1
Hutchison Drive	D2
Irvinebank Road	D3
James Baird Court	B3
Jamieson Road	C1
John Morton Crescent	D2
Kirkland Close	D2
Kirkland Park Court	D2
Kirkland Park Gardens	D2
Kirkland Road	D2
Lace Mill Wynd	C2
Laggan View	E2
Lanfine Quadrant	B3
Lanfine View	B3
Lintmill Road	A3
Lochore Terrace	B2
Loudoun Court	C2
McIlroy Court	D2
Mclauchlan Court	C3
Mairs Road	C3
Manse Brae	E2
Matthaburn Lane	C2
Morton Court	C3
Morton Park Drive	B3
Muir Drive	A3
Murdoch Road	D2
New Street	B2
Paterson Terrace	D2
Paton Drive	C1
Quoiting Green Road	B2
Ranoldcoup Road	C3
Richmond Gardens	C3
Robertson Gardens	D2
Roxburgh Gardens	B3
Sim Gardens	C3
Station Gate	C2
Temple Street	C3
West Donington Street	C2
West Edith Street	B3
West Main Street	B3
Woodburn Court	B2
Earl Crescent	C3
Earl Drive	C2
Earl Mount	C2
Earl Rise	C2, C3
Fullerton Avenue	C2
Gulliland Avenue	C2
Kilmarnock Road	C2
Kilnford Crescent	A2
Kilnford Drive	B2
Laurieston Court	C3
Lochside Court	C3
Main Street	C2
Merkland Park	C3
Merkland Place	C3
Newfield Drive	C2
Newfield Place	C2
Old Auchans View	B2
Old Loans Road	C3
Parkthorn View	B2
Richmond Lane	C3
Richmond Terrace	C3
School Wynd	C2
Stuart Place	C2
Tarbolton Road	C3
Troon Road	A2
Vernon Place	B2
Wallace Avenue	C2
Warly Drive	C3
Warly Place	C3
Wilson Place	B2
Winehouse Yett	B2

Index to Dundonald

Auchans Avenue	B2
Auchans Drive	B2
Beaton Lane	D3
Bruce Avenue	C2
Castle Drive	C2
Castleview	B1, C1
Coats Place	B2
Cochrane Avenue	C2
Cochrane Drive	B2
Drybridge Road	B2

Index to Drybridge

Dreghorn Road	A1
Griers Walk	A1
Main Street	A1
Shewalton Drive	A1
Shewalton Moss	A1
Shewalton Road	A1
Station Row	B1

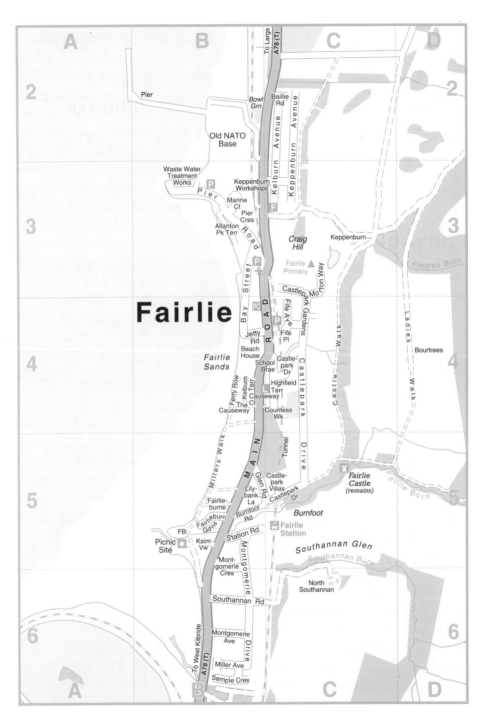

Fairlie

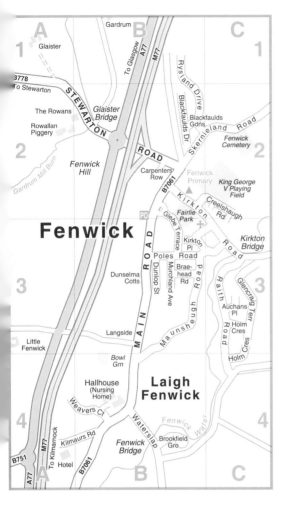

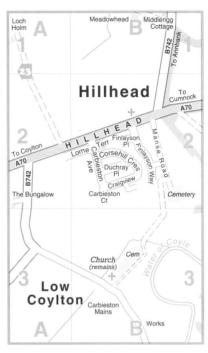

Index to Hillhead

Carbieston Avenue	B2	Finlayson Place	B2
Carbieston Court	B2	Finlayson Way	B2
Corsehill Crescent	B2	Hillhead	A2
Craigview	B2	Lorne Terrace	B2
Duchray Place	B2	Manse Road	B2

Index to Fairlie

		Glen Road	B5	School Brae	C4
		Highfield Terrace	C4	Semple Crescent	B6
Allanton Park Terrace	B3	Jetty Road	B4	Southannan Road	B6
Baillie Road	C2	Kaim View	B5	Station Road	B5
Bay Street	B4	Kelburn Avenue	C3		
Beach House	B4	Kelburn Terrace	B4		
Burnfoot Road	B5	Keppenburn Avenue	C3	**Index to Fenwick**	
Castle Walk	C4	Ladies Walk	D4		
Castlepark Drive	C4	Lilybank Lane	B5	Auchans Place	C3
Castlepark Gardens	C4	Main Road	B5	Blackfaulds Drive	B2
Castlepark Villas	C5	Marine Court	B3	Blackfaulds Gardens	B2
Causeway Court	B4	Miller Avenue	B6	Braehead Road	B3
Causeway, The	B4	Millers Walk	B5	Brookfield Grove	B4
Countess Walk	C4	Montgomerie Avenue	B6	Carpenters Row	B2
Fairlieburne Gardens	B5	Montgomerie Crescent	B5	Creelshaugh Road	C2
Fairlieburne	B5	Montgomerie Drive	B5	Dunlop Street	B3
Ferry Row	B4	Morton Way	C3	Dunselma Cottages	B3
Fife Avenue	C4	Pier Crescent	B3	Glebe Terrace	B2
Fife Place	C4	Pier Road	B3		

Glencraig Terrace	C3
Holm Crescent	C4
Kilmaurs Road	A4
Kirkton Place	B3
Kirkton Road	C2
Main Road	B3
Maunsheugh Road	B3
Murchland Avenue	B3
Poles Road	B3
Raith Road	C3
Rysland Drive	B1
Skernieland Road	B2
Stewarton Road	A2
Waterslap	B4
Weavers Court	B4

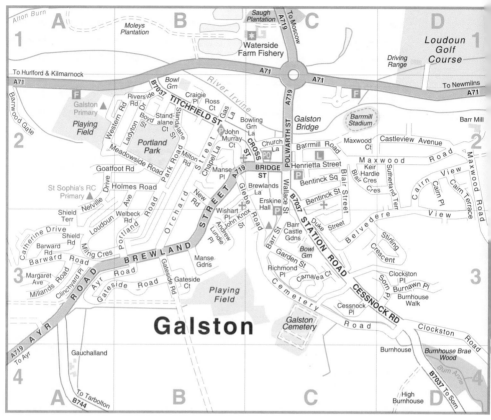

Galston

Index to Galston

		Church Lane	C2	New Road	B2
		Clinchyard Place	A3	Orchard Street	B3
Andrew Lundie Place	B3	Clockston Place	D3	Park Road	B2
Ayr Road	A3	Clockston Road	D3	Polwarth Street	C2
Barr Castle Gardens	C3	Craigie Place	B2	Portland Road	B3
Barr Street	C3	Cross Street	C2	Richmond Place	C3
Barrmill Road	C2	Duke Street	C3	Riverside Road	B2
Barward Road	A3	Erskine Hall	C2	Ross Court	B2
Barwood Gate	A2	Garden Street	C3	Shield Road	A3
Belvedere View	C3	Gas Lane	B2	Shield Terrace	A3
Bentinck Square	C2	Gateside Court	B3	Sorn Place	D3
Bentinck Street	C2	Gateside Road	B3	Standalane Court	B2
Blair Crescent	C2	Glebe Road	B2	Standalane Street	B2
Blair Street	C2	Goatfoot Road	A2	Station Road	C3
Bowling Green Lane	C2	Henrietta Street	C2	Stirling Crescent	D3
Boyd Street	B2	Holmes Road	B2	Sutherland Terrace	D2
Brewlands Lane	C2	John Knox Street	B3	Titchfield Street	B2
Brewland Street	B3	John Murray Court	B2	Wallace Street	C2
Bridge Street	C2	Keir Hardie Crescent	C2	Welbeck Road	B3
Burnawn Place	D3	Ladyton Drive	B2	Western Road	A2
Burnhouse Walk	D3	Loudoun Avenue	A3	Wishart Place	B3
Cairn Place	D2	Manse Gardens	B3		
Cairn Terrace	D2	Manse Place	B2	**Index to Girvan**	
Cairn View	D2	Margaret Avenue	A3		
Carnalea Court	C3	Maxwood Court	C2	Ailsa Place	B3
Castleview Avenue	D2	Maxwood Road	C2, D2	Ailsa Street East	B3
Catherine Drive	A3	Meadowside Road	B2	Ailsa Street West	A3
Cemetery Road	C3	Millands Road	A3	Ainslie Road	A5
Cessnock Place	C3	Milrig Crescent	A3	Ardmillan Road	C2
Cessnock Road	C3	Milton Road	B2	Arran Court	B4
Chapel Lane	B2	Nelville Drive	A2	Arran View	A2

Avenue, The	C3
Assel Place	C4
Ballochtoul	C4
Ballybroke Street	A4
Bay Terrace	A5
Beech Way	B5
Bennane Road	A5
Birch Terrace	B5
Bourtreehall	B2
Boyle Court	B2
Bridge Street	B2
Byne Cottages	B6
Byne Court	C4
Carrick Street	B2
Cauldshore	A5
Chalmers Arcade	B3
Chalmers Court (1)	B3
Cherry Drive	B5
Chestnut Drive	B4
Church Square	B2
Clyde View	C3
Coalpots Road	C4
Connor Court	C3
Craig Court	B3
Cuddieston	C4
Dalrymple Street	B4
Deacons Place	B3
Doune Street	A4
Douneburn Crescent	A5
Downhill Road	B4
continued overleaf...

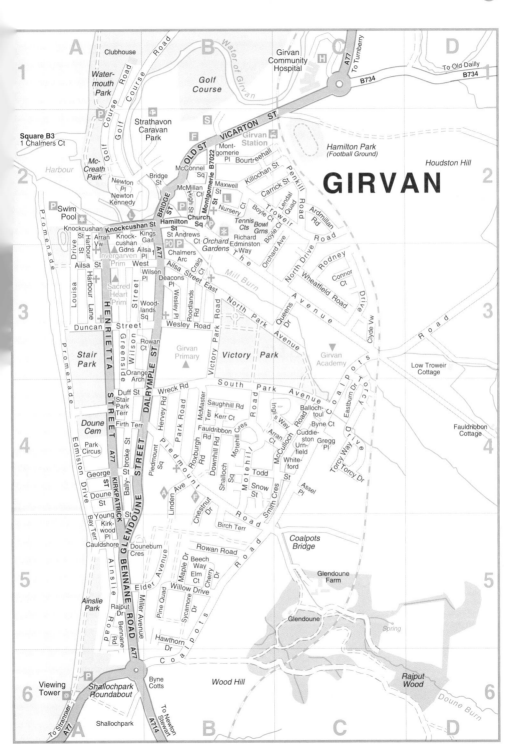

GIRVAN

Index to Girvan

continued from overleaf...

Duff Street	A4
Duncan Street	A3
Eastburn Drive	C4
Edmiston Drive	A4
Elder Avenue	B5
Elm Court	B5
Fauldribbon Road	B4
Firth Terrace	A4
George Street	A4
Glendoune Street	A4
Golf Course Road	A2
Greenside	A3
Gregg Place	C4
Hamilton Street	B2
Harbour Lane	A3
Harbour Street	A3
Hawthorn Drive	B5
Henrietta Street	A3
Hervey Road	B4
High Street	B2
Inglis Way	C4
Kerr Court	B4
Killochan Street	B2
Kings Gait	B2
Kirkpatrick Street	A4
Kirkwood Place	A5
Knockcushan Street	A2
Knockcushan Gardens	A2
Lendal Quadrant	C2
Linden Avenue	B4
Louisa Drive	A3
McConnel Square	B2
McCulloch Road	C4
McMaster Terrace	B4
McMillan Court	B2

Maple Drive	B5
Maxwell Street	B2
Miller Avenue	A5
Montgomerie Place	B2
Montgomerie Street	B2
Motehill Crescent	B4
Motehill Road	B4
Newton Kennedy	A2
Newton Place	A2
North Drive	C3
North Park Avenue	B3
Nursery Court	B2
Old Street	B2
Orange Arch	A3
Orchard Avenue	B3
Park Circus	A4
Park Road	B4
Penkill Road	C2
Piedmount Road	B4
Piedmount Square	B4
Pine Quadrant	B5
Promenade	A3
Queens Drive	C3
Rajput Drive	A5
Richard Edminston Way	B3
Rodney Drive	C3
Roodlands Road	B3
Rowan Court	A3
Rowan Road	B5
Roxburgh Road	B4
St Andrews Court	B2
Saughhill Road	B4
Shalloch Square	B4
Smith Crescent	B4
Snow Street	B4
South Park Avenue	B4
Stair Park Terrace	A4

Sycamore Drive	B5
Todd Street	B4
Torcy Drive	C4
Torcy Way	C4
Troweir Road	B2
Urnfield	C4
Vicarton Street	B2
Victory Park Road	B3
Wesley Place	B3
Wesley Road	B3
Wheatfield Road	C3
Whitefield	C4
Willow Drive	B5
Wilson Place	A3
Wilson Street	A3
Woodlands Square	B3
Wreck Road	B4
Young Street	A5

Index to Hurlford

Academy Court	B3
Academy Street	B3
Ashton Drive	C4
Barleith Court	C4
Barnweil Drive	B4
Bellfield Avenue	A3
Bellfield Court	A3
Blair Avenue	B3
Blair Crescent	B3
Blair Road	B3
Cessnock Avenue	C4
Cessnock Drive	C4
Cessnock Gardens	C3
Cessnock Road	C3
Craigie Road	C4

Cross, The	C3
Drumleyhill Drive	C4
Dykehead Drive	C4
Furnace Court	B3
Galston Road	C3
Graham Court	B3
Holyoake Court	C2
Kaimshill Cottages	A3
Kerrmuir Avenue	C4
Kersland Crescent	B3
Knowehead Road	C4
Leven Court	C3
Leven Drive	C3
Lifnock Avenue	C3
Lomond Avenue	C3
Main Road	A2
Marchmont Court	C2
Mauchline Road	C3
Maxwell Gardens	B3
Mayfield Avenue	D4
Morris Crescent	B3
Moss Court	C4
Ness Gardens	C3
Portland Court	B3
Portland Brae	B2
Reid Court	B2
Riccarton Road	A3
Riccarton Mill Cottages	A3
Richardson Avenue	D4
Roxburgh Road	B2
Salisbury Avenue	C2
Sherwood Road	C3
Station Drive	A3
Union Street	B3
Walden Road	B3
Walker Court	C3
Wallace Court	A3

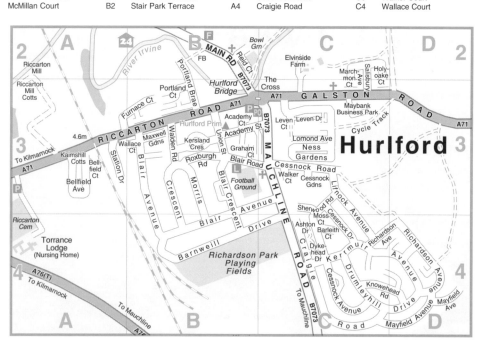

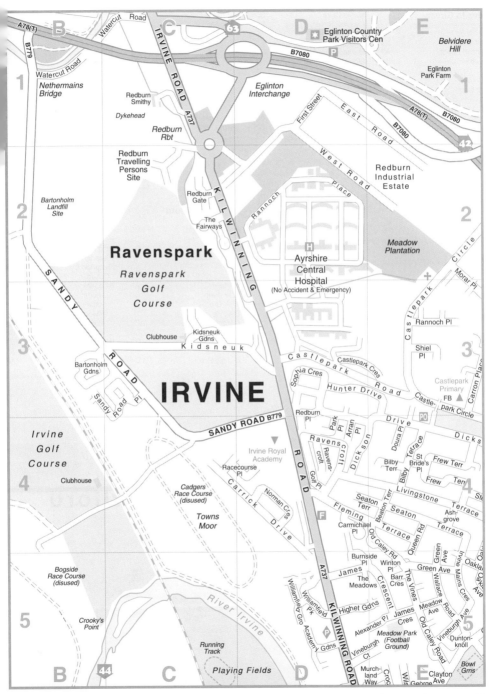

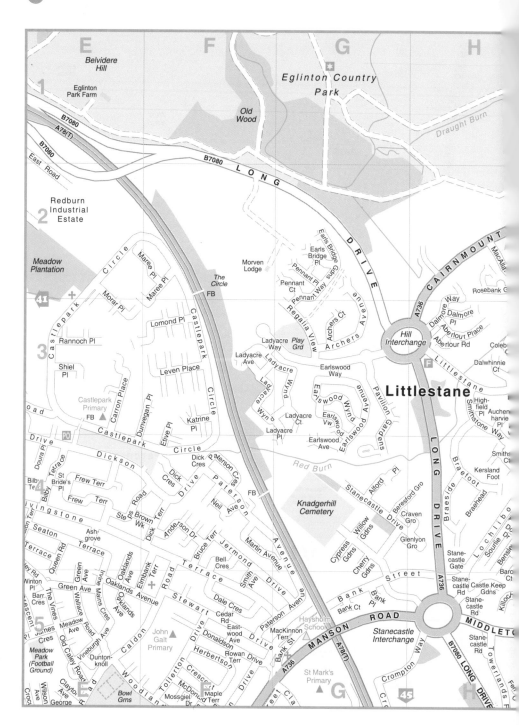

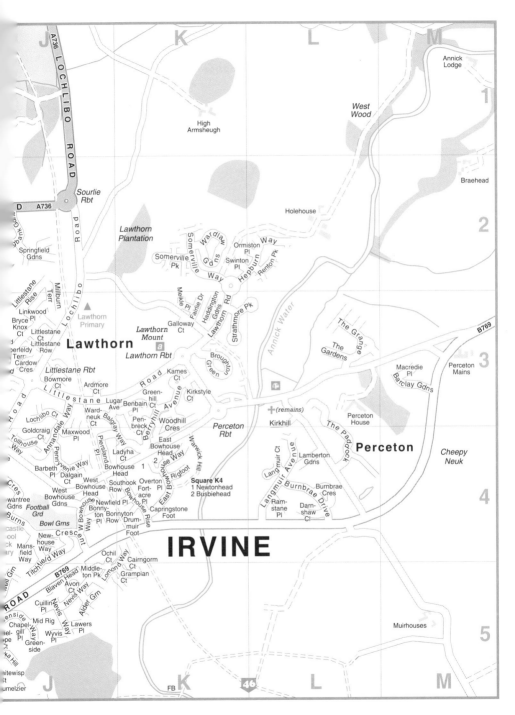

Annick Lodge

West Wood

Braehead

1

Sourlie Rbt

D A736

Holehouse

2

Springfield Gdns

Lawthorn Plantation

Somerville Pk

Somerville Way

Wardlaw Gdns

Ormiston Pl

Swinton Pl

Hepburn

Renton Pk

Way

Annick Water

High Armsheugh

Littlestane Rise

Millburn Terr

Linkwood Pl

Bryce Knox Ct

Littlestane Ct

Littlestane Row

erfeldy Terr

Cardow Cres

Lawthorn Primary

Meikle Pl

Fairlie Dr

Haddington Gdns

Strathmore Pk

Lawthorn Rd

Lawthorn Mount

Galloway Ct

Lawthorn

Lawthorn Rbt

Broughton Green

The Grange

The Gardens

Macredie Pl

Barclay Gdns

B769

Perceton Mains

3

Littlestane Rbt

Bowmore Ct

Ardmore Ct

Road

Kames Ct

(remains)

Kirkhill

Perceton House

Greenhill Ct

Kirkstyle Ct

Lugar Ave

Benbain Pl

Littlestane

Road

Lochlibo Ct

Ward-neuk Ct

Balgray Way

Berryhill Ave

Penbreck Ct

Woodhill Cres

Perceton Rbt

Kirkhill

The Paddock

Perceton House

Perceton

Cheepy Neuk

Goldcraig Ct

Maxwood Pl

Annandale Way

Piersland

Ladyha Ct

East Bowhouse Head

Warwick Hill

Langmuir Ct

Langmuir Avenue

Lamberton Gdns

4

Tollhouse Way

Pennyvenie Way

Barbeth Pl

Dalgain Ct

West Bowhouse Head

Bowhouse Head

1

2

East Bowhouse Way

Square K4
1 Newtonhead
2 Busbiehead

Burnbrae Cres

Ram-stane Pl

Darn-shaw Cl

Burnbrae Drive

wantree Gdns

Burns

West Bowhouse Gdns

Southook Row

Newfield Pl

Bonny-ton Pl

Overton Fort-acre Pl

Bonnyton Row

Bowhouse Rise

East Rigfoot

Capringstone Foot

castle ool ck ary

Bowl Grns

New-house Way

Cres-cent

Drum-muir Foot

IRVINE

Mans-field Way

Football Grd

Titchfield Way

B769

Blaven Head

Ochil Ct

Middle-ton Pk

Lomond Way

Cairngorm Ct

Grampian Ct

Gm

Avon Pl

Nevis Way

Alder Grn

Cuillin Pl

Nevis Pl

Lawers Pl

Muirhouses

5

Chapel-gill

Mid Rig

Wyvis Pl

Green-side

el-pe

s Hill

itewisp st umelzier

ROAD

Index to street names can be found starting on page 96

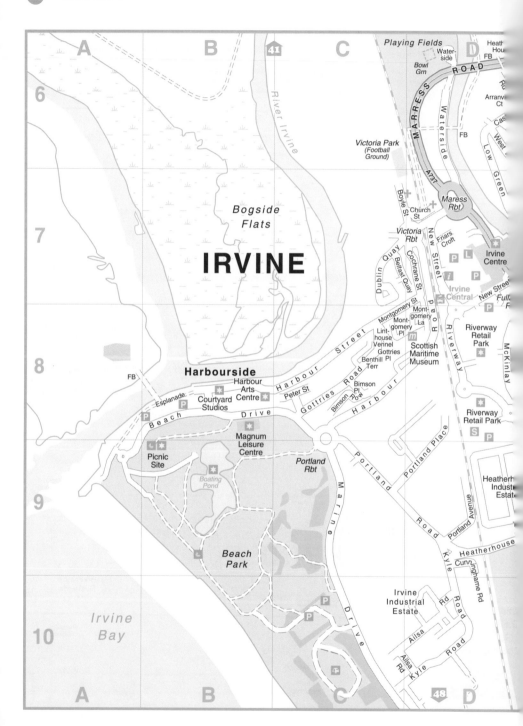

IRVINE

Bogside Flats

Playing Fields

Victoria Park
(Football Ground)

Maress Rbt

Victoria Rbt

Irvine Centre

Irvine Central

Dublin Quay

Belfast Quay

Cochrane St

New Street

Church St

Boyle St

Friars Croft

Riverway Retail Park

Montgomery St

Montgomery La

Montgomery Pl

Linthouse Vennel

Gottries Pl

Benthill Terr

Bimson Pl

Bimson Row

Scottish Maritime Museum

Harbour Street

Gottries Road

Harbour

Peter St

Harbourside

FB

Esplanade

Harbour Arts Centre

Courtyard Studios

Beach Drive

Magnum Leisure Centre

Picnic Site

Boating Pond

Beach Park

Portland Rbt

Portland

Marine Drive

Portland Place

Portland Road

Riverway Retail Park

McKinlay

Heatherh Indust Estate

Irvine Industrial Estate

Heatherhouse

Kyle Road

Cunninghame Rd

Ailsa Rd

Kyle Road

Ailsa Rd

Irvine Bay

MARESS ROAD

Waterside

Bowl Grn

Heath Hou

Arranvi Ct

Low Green

West

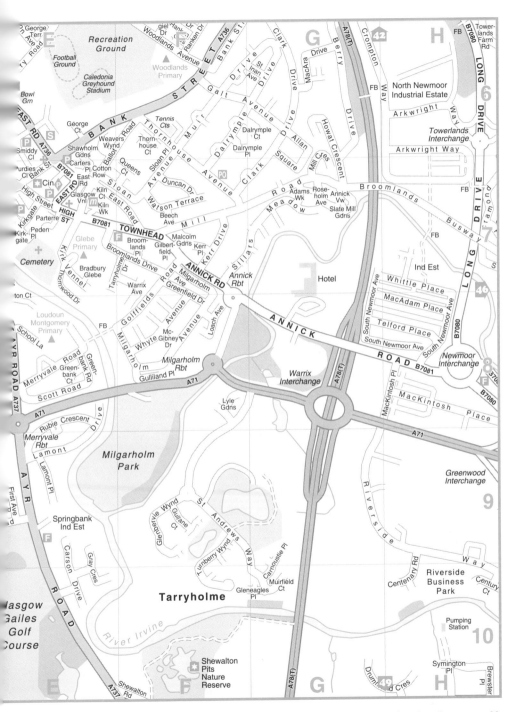

Index to street names can be found starting on page 96

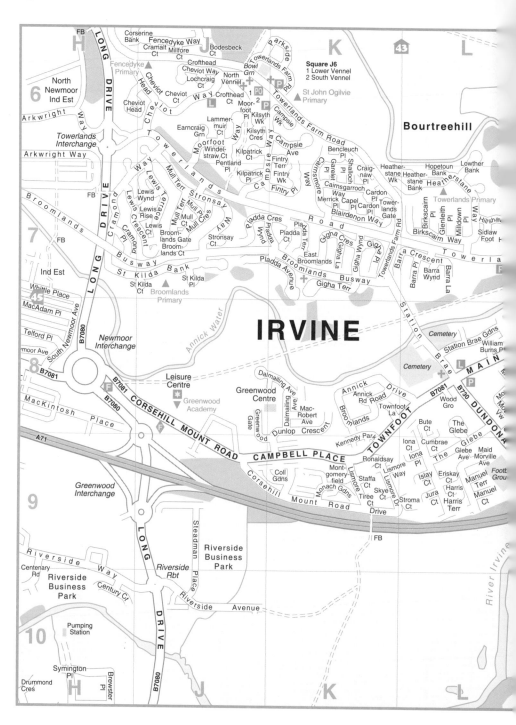

IRVINE

Bourtreehill

Square J6
1 Lower Vennel
2 South Vennel

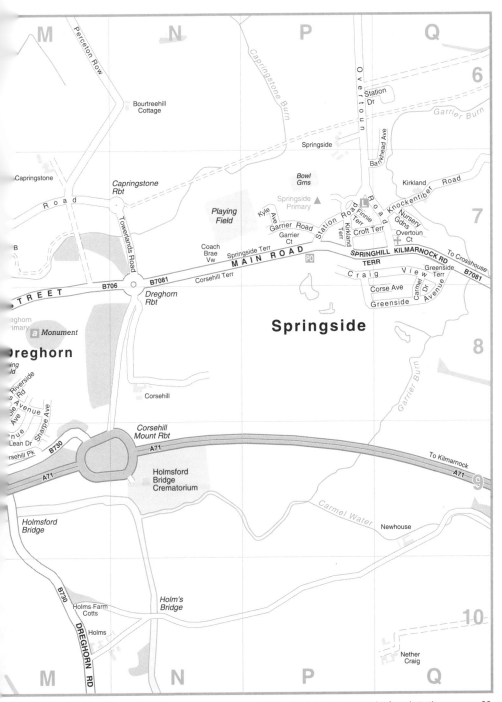

M N P Q

Perceton Row

Capringstone Burn

6

Overtoun

Station Dr

Garrier Burn

Bourtreehill Cottage

Bankhead Ave

Springside

Bankhead

Capringstone

Capringstone Rbt

Bowl Grns

Kirkland Road

Knockentiber Road

Road

Towerlands Road

Playing Field

Springside Primary

Kyle Ave

Garrier Road

Garrier Ct

Station Road

Finnie Terr

Kirkland Terr

Croft Terr

Nursery Gdns

Overtoun Ct

7

B

Coach Brae Vw

Springside Terr

MAIN ROAD

PO

SPRINGHILL TERR

KILMARNOCK RD

To Crosshouse

B706

B7081

Corsehill Terr

Craig View

Greenside Terr

B7081

STREET

Dreghorn Rbt

Corse Ave

Carmel Dr

Avenue

Greenside

reghorn rimary

a Monument

Springside

Garrier Burn

8

Dreghorn

ing ld

Riverside Rd

Avenue

Sharpe Ave

Corsehill

Lean Dr

rsehill Pk

B730

Corsehill Mount Rbt

A71

To Kilmarnock

A71

A71

Holmsford Bridge Crematorium

9

Holmsford Bridge

Carmel Water

Newhouse

B730

Holms Farm Cotts

Holm's Bridge

10

DREGHORN RD

Holms

Nether Craig

M N P Q

Index to street names can be found starting on page 96

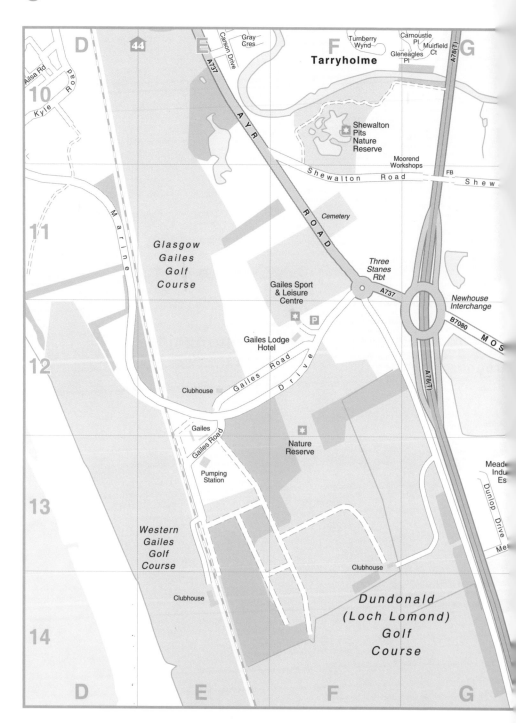

D

E

Gray
Cres

Carson Drive

A737

F

Turnberry
Wynd

Carnoustie
Pl

Gleneagles
Pl

Muirfield
Ct

G

A78(T)

Tarryholme

Allsa Rd

R
o
a
d

Kyle

A
Y
R

10

Shewalton
Pits
Nature
Reserve

Moorend
Workshops

FB

S h e w

Shewalton Road

M
a
r
i
n
e

R
O
A
D

Cemetery

11

Glasgow
Gailes
Golf
Course

Three
Stanes
Rbt

A737

Newhouse
Interchange

B7080

M O S

Gailes Sport
& Leisure
Centre

P

Gailes Lodge
Hotel

Gailes Road

D
r
i
v
e

A78(T)

12

Clubhouse

Gailes

Gailes Road

Nature
Reserve

Mead
Indu
Es

Pumping
Station

Dunlop Drive

Me

13

Western
Gailes
Golf
Course

Clubhouse

Clubhouse

Clubhouse

*Dundonald
(Loch Lomond)
Golf
Course*

14

D

E

F

G

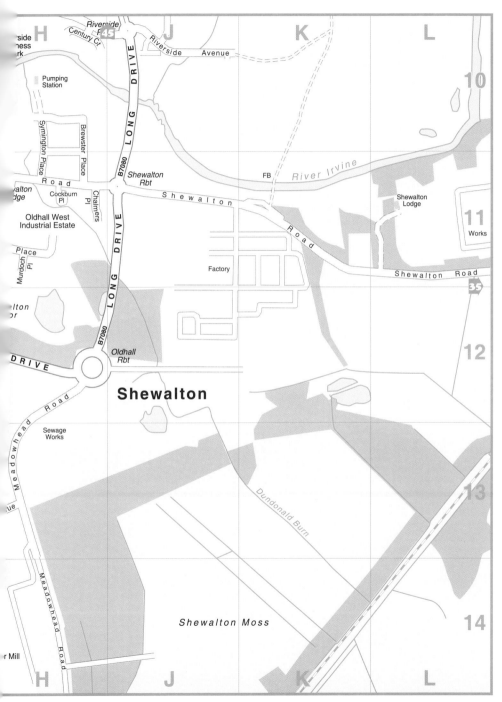

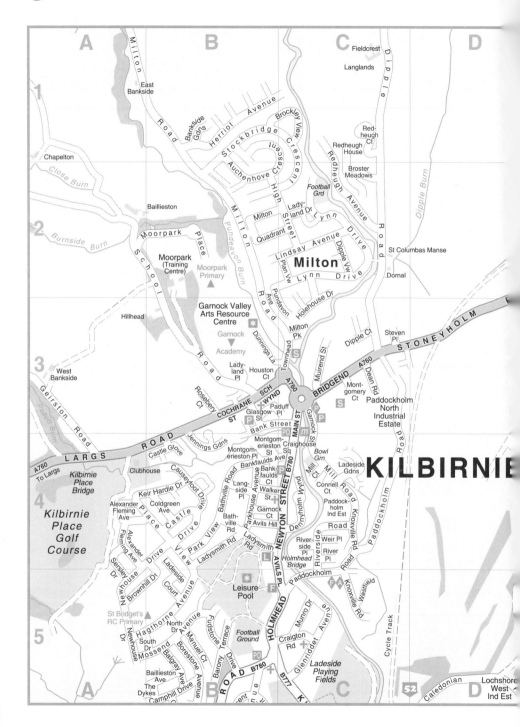

KILBIRNIE

Milton

Kilbirnie Place Golf Course

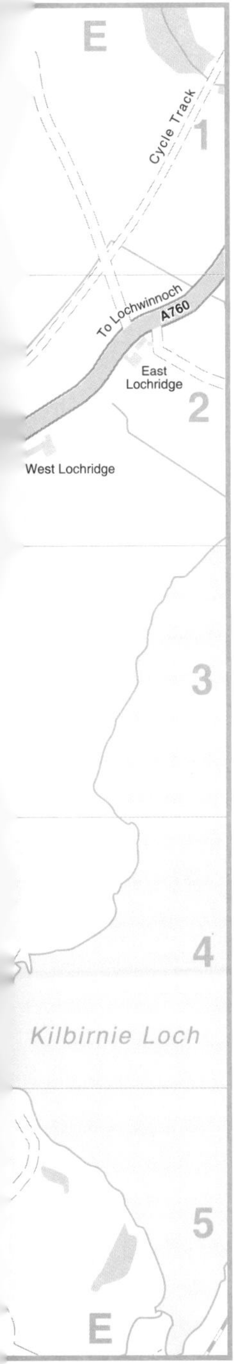

E

1

Cycle Track

To Lochwinnoch A760

East Lochridge

West Lochridge

2

3

Kilbirnie Loch

4

5

E

Index to Kilbirnie

Alexander Fleming Avenue	A4	Kersland Road	D7
Auchengree Road	E7	Kerswinning Avenue	B6
Auchenhove Crescent	B2	Kirkland Road	C6
Avils Hill	B4	Knoxville Road	C4, C5
Avils Place	C5	Ladeside Court	B4, B5
Baillieston Avenue	B5	Ladeside Gardens	C4
Balgray Avenue	B5	Ladyland Drive	C2
Balgray Road	C6	Ladyland Place	B3
Bank Street	B3	Ladysmith Road	B4
Bankfaulds Avenue	B4	Langside Place	B4
Bankfaulds Court	B4	Largs Road	A4
Bankside Gardens	B1	Lindsay Avenue	C2
Barony Terrace	B5	Loadingbank Court	B6
Bathville Road	B4	Loadingbank	B6
Beith Road	D7	Lochend Road	D6
Borestone Avenue	B6	Longbar Avenue	E7
Bridgend	C3	Lynn Drive	C2
Briery Court	B6	Main Road	C7
Brockley View	C1	Main Street	C4
Broster Meadows	C2	Manuel Court	B5
Brownhill Drive	A5	Mill Court	C4
Burnside Street	C7	Mill Road	C4
Caledonian Place	C6	Milton Park	C3
Caledonian Road	D6	Milton Quadrant	B2
Camphill Drive	B5	Milton Road	A1, B2
Castle Drive	B4	Montgomerieston Place	B4
Castle Grove	B4	Montgomerieston Street	B4
Causeyfoot Drive	B4	Montgomery Court	C3
Central Avenue	B6	Moorpark Place	A2
Cochrane Street	B3	Mossend Avenue	B5
Coldgreen Avenue	B4	Muirend Street	C3
Connell Court	C4	Munro Drive	C5
Craigends Road	C7	Newhouse Drive	A5
Craighouse Square	C4	Newton Street	C4
Craigton Road	C5	North Drive	B5
Daisybank	D7	Paddockholm Road	C5
Dalry Road	B6, A7	Paduff Place	B3
Davidson Avenue	E7	Park View	B4
Dean Road	C3	Parkhouse Avenue	B4
Dennyholm Wynd	C4	Place View	B4
Dipple Court	C3	Plan View	C2
Dipple Road	C1	Pundavon Avenue	B2
Dipple View	C2	Redheugh Avenue	C1
Dunnings Lane	B3	Redheugh Court	C1
Dykes, The	B5	Redheugh House	C1
Eastern Crescent	B6	River Place	C4
Fudstone Drive	B5	Riverside Place	C4
Garnock Court	B4	Riverside Road	C4
Garnock Street	C3	Rosebery Court	B3
Garnock View	C6	St Brennans Court	B6
Garnockside	C7	School Road	A2
Geirston Road	A3	School Wynd	B3
Glasgow Street	B3	Sersley Drive	A4
Glebe Road	C6	South Drive	B5
Glenriddet Avenue	C5	South Neuk	B6
Grahamston Avenue	C6	Station Court	D7
Greenside Avenue	B6	Steven Place	C3
Hagthorne Avenue	B5	Stockbridge Crescent	B1
Herriot Avenue	B1	Stoneyholm Road	C3
High Street	C2	Sunderland Court	B6
Holehouse Drive	C3	Townhead	C3
Holmhead	B5	Walker Street	B4
Holms Road	C7	Weir Place	C4
Houston Court	B3	Western Crescent	B6
Janefield Place	C6	Westfield	C5
Jennings Gardens	B4		
Keir Hardie Drive	B4		
Kersland Place	D7		

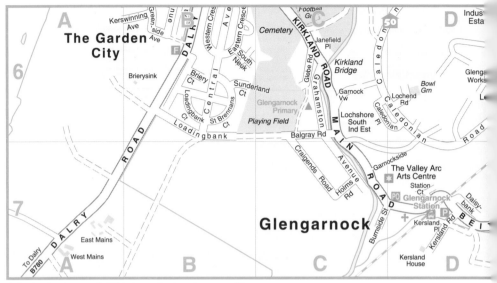

Index to street names in Kilbirnie can be found on page 51

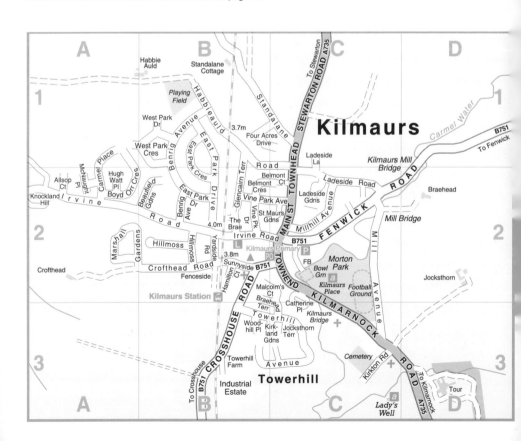

Kirkmichael

Aitkenhead

Index to Kilmaurs

Allsop Court	A2	Kirkton Road	C3
Beaufield Gardens	B2	Knockland Hill	A2
Belmont Court	C2	Ladeside Gardens	C2
Belmont Crescent	C2	Ladeside Lane	C1
Benrig Avenue	B2	Ladeside Road	C2
Boyd Orr Crescent	A2	McNaught Place	A2
Brae, The	B2	Main Street	C2
Braehead Terrace	B2	Malcolm's Court	C2
Carmel Place	A2	Marshall Gardens	A2
Catherine Place	C3	Mill Avenue	C2
Crofthead Road	B2	Millhill Avenue	C2
Crosshouse Road	B3	St Maurs Gardens	C2
East Park Crescent	B1	Standalane	B1
East Park Drive	B1	Stewarton Road	C1
Fenwick Road	C2	Sunnyside	B2
Four Acres Drive	B1	Towerhill Avenue	B3
Glencairn Terrace	B2	Townend	C2
Habbieauld Road	B1	Townhead	C2
Hamilton Court	B2	Vine Park Avenue	B2
Hillmoss	B2	Vine Park Drive	B2
Hugh Watt Place	A2	West Park Crescent	B1
Irvine Road	B2	West Park Drive	B1
Jocksthorn Terrace	C3	Woodhill Place	B3
Kilmarnock Road	C2	Yardside Road	B2
Kirkland Gardens	B3		

Index to Kirkmichael

Barganock Road	B2
Bolestyle Crescent	B2
Bolestyle Road	B2
Burnside Row	B2
Dalrymple Road	B1
Dyrock Road	B2
Maybole Road	A2
Meadowbank Place	B2
Patna Road	B2, C1
Portcheek Terrace	B2
Straiton Road	B2
Woodside Avenue	B2

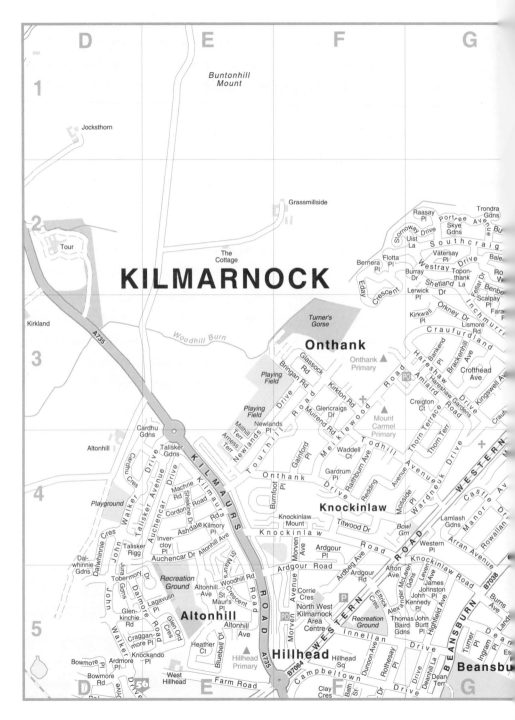

KILMARNOCK

Buntonhill Mount

Jocksthorn

Grassmillside

The Cottage

Kirkland

Tour

A735

Woodhill Burn

Turner's Gorse

Onthank

Onthank Primary

Raasay Pl
Trondra Gdns
Stornoway Drive
Portree Avenue
Skye Gdns
Uist La
Southcraig
Vatersay Pl
Flotta Pl
Westray Drive
Bale
Bernera Pl
Burray Dr
Topon-thank
Ro
Eday
Shetland La
Benbe
Crescent
Lerwick Pl
Scalpay Pl
Fara
Kirkwall Pl
Orkney Dr
Inchmurr
Lismore Rd
Craufurdland
Bankend Pl
Hareshaw
Brackenhill Ave
Crofthead Ave
Hareshaw Gardens
Kingswell Ave
Amlaird Road
Creigton Ct
Crau

Glassock Rd
Bringan Rd
Playing Field
Kirkton Rd
Meiklewood Road
PO
Thorn Terrace Road
Thorn Terr
Thorn Terr

Playing Field
Millhill Terr
Newlands Pl
Glencraigs Dr
Muirend Rd
Mount Carmel Primary

Cardhu Gdns
Altonhill
Talisker Gdns
Cardhu Cres
Walker Drive
Machrie Rd
Kilmaurs Road
Shiskine Rd
Kilmory Pl
Ashdale Rd
Newlands Terr
Arness Terr
Tournhill Drive
Newlands
Gainford Pl
Waddell Ct
Gardrum Pl
Todhill Avenue
Avenueuk Drive
Wardneuk Drive
WESTERN

Playground
Auchencar Drive
Cordons
Onthank Drive
Redding
Mosside
Castle Av

Dalwhinnie Cres
Talisker Rigg
Inver-cloy Pl
Auchencar Dr
Altonhill Ave
Burnfoot Pl
Knockinlaw Mount
Knockinlaw
Titwood Dr
Bowl Grn
Lamlash Gdns
Manor Dr
Rowallan

John Walker
Tobermory Dr
Jura Gdns
Recreation Ground
Altonhill Ave
Woodhill Rd
St Maur's Crescent
Knockinlaw Road
Western Ave
Knockinlaw Road
Arran Avenue
B7038

Dal-whinnie Gdns
Lagavulin Pl
Morven Ave
Ardgour Pl
Ardbeg Ave
Afton Ave
Alexander McLaren Gdns
James Johnston Pl
Burns Ave

Glen-kinchie Rd
Dalmore Road
Glen Ord Cres
Ardgour Road
Morven Avenue
Corrie Cres
Ardgour Rd
Ettrick Cres
John Kennedy Pl
Thomas Baird Gdns
John Burtt Gdns
Dean

Altonhill
Craggan-more Pl
Knockando Pl
Heather Ct
Bluebell Rd
Altonhill Ave
North West Kilmarnock Area Centre
PO
Recreation Ground
Highfield Rd
Innellan Drive
BEANSBURN
Ingram

Bowmore Pl
Ardmore Pl
West Hillhead
Hillhead Primary
Hillhead
Hillhead Sq
Dunoon Dr
Rothesay Dr
Deanhill La
Dean Terr
Beansbu

Bowmore Rd
56
Farm Road
A735
B7064
Campbeltown
Clay Cres
Bath St
WESTERN ROAD

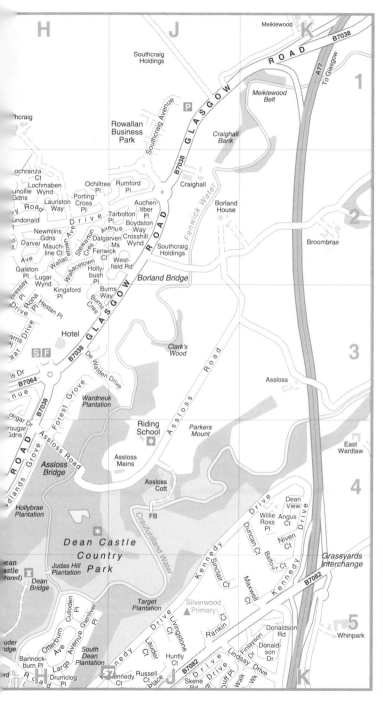

Index to Kilmarnock

Aberfeldy Place	B8
Academy Apartments	G8
Academy Street	F10
Afton Avenue	F5
Ailsa Place	H3
Aird Avenue	E9
Alder Place	D8
Alexander McLaren	F5
Gardens	
Alloway Avenue	H8
Almond Place	D8
Altonhill Avenue	E5
Amlaird Road	G3
Anderson Place	K6
Angus Court	K4
Annan Court	G11
Annan Road	G11
Annanhill Avenue	C7
Annanhill House	C8
Annick Place	G11
Arbuckle Street	G8
Ardbeg Avenue	F5
Ardgour Place	F4
Ardgour Road	F5
Ardle Avenue	H11
Ardmore Place	D5
Armour Street	F9
Armstrong Road	J6
Arness Terrace	E4
Arran Avenue	G4
Arrothill Drive	D9
Ash Place	D9
Ashdale Road	E4
Assloss Road	H4
Auchencar Drive	E4
Auchentiber Place	J2
Avon Place	H11
Ayr Road	E13
Bailiehill Place	D7
Baird Place	H6
Baird Road	H6
Baleshrae Crescent	G2
Balfour Court	K5
Balgray Avenue	F14
Ballochmyle Walk	B9
Balmoral Road	E6
Balvenie Drive	D6
Bank Place	F8
Bank Street	F8
Bankend Place	G3
Bannerman Drive	K6
Bannockburn Place	H5
Barassie Place	E12
Barbadoes Place	E10
Barbadoes Road	E10
Barclay Drive	J6
Barnweil Road	E11
Bath Street	F5
Beansburn	G5
Beauly Crescent	G11
Beech Avenue	D8
Belleisle Place	E12
Bellevue Gardens	D7
Bellevue Road	D7
Bellfield Avenue	K10
Bellfield Court	K10
Bellsland Drive	F10
Bellsland Grove	F10
Bellsland Place	F9
Benbecula Road	G2
Bentinck Street	F9
Bernera Place	F2
Birch Place	D8
Blacksyke Avenue	E13
Blackwood Avenue	E10
Blair Street	F6

continued on page 58...

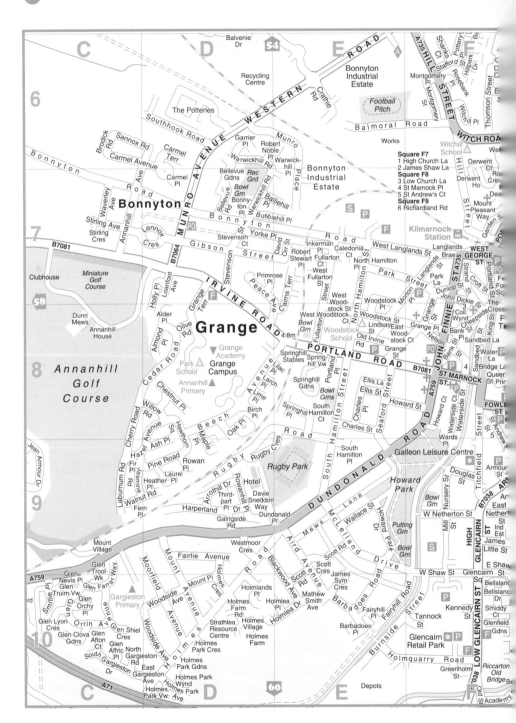

Square F7
1 High Church La
2 James Shaw La
Square F8
3 Low Church La
4 St Marnock Pl
5 St Andrew's Ct
Square F9
6 Richardland Rd

Bonnyton

Grange

Grange Campus

Annanhill Golf Course

Rugby Park

Howard Park

Galleon Leisure Centre

Glencairn Retail Park

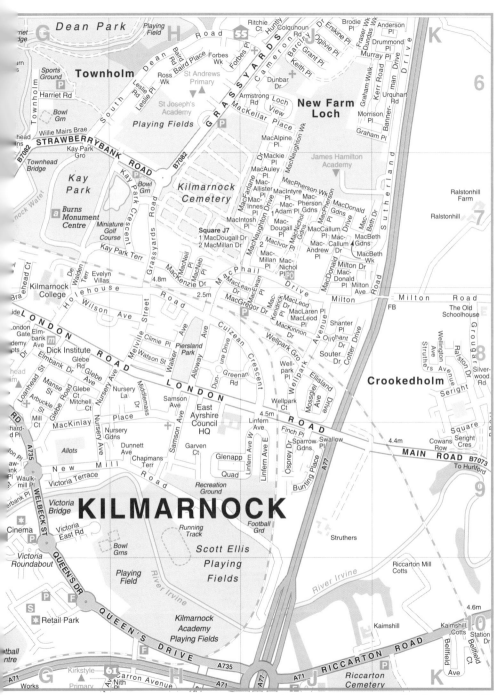

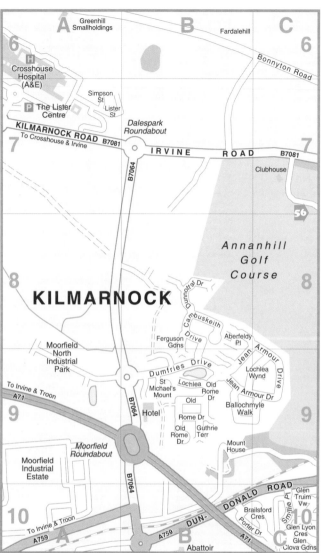

Carmel Place	
Carmel Terrace	
Carron Avenue	G11,
Castle Drive	
Cedar Road	
Central Avenue	
Cessock Place	
Chapmans Terrace	
Charles Place	
Charles Street	
Cheapside Street	
Cherry Road	
Chestnut Place	
Cheviot Place	G
Church Lane	F
Church Street	
Clark Street	
Clay Crescent	
Clayslaps View	H
Climie Place	
Clyde Place	G
College Wynd	
Colonsay Place	
Colquhoun Road	
Commonhead Road	F
Cordon Road	E
Corrie Crescent	F
Cotter Drive	
Cowans Row	K
Cragganmore Place	D
Craigie Avenue	F1
Craigie Place	F1
Craigie Road	F1
Crathie Road	E
Craufurdland Road	G
Creigton Court	G
Criffel Place	G1
Croe Place	G1
Croft Street	F
Crofthead Avenue	G
Cromdale Road	G12
Cross, The	F
Crosshill Wynd	J
Crosshouse Road	A
Cruachan Place	H12
Cuillin Place	G13
Culloden Place	H5
Culzean Crescent	J8
Cumbrae Drive	H3
Cunninghame Drive	E12
Cuthbert Place	G6
Dalgarven Mews	J2
Dalmore Road	D5
Dalwhinnie Crescent	D5
Dalwhinnie Gardens	D5
Damhead Road	E13
Danny Coffey Avenue	F6
Darnley Drive	E11
Darvel Avenue	H2
Davaar Drive	H3
David Orr Street	E7
Davie Sneddon Way	D9
De Walden Drive	H3
De Walden Terrace	G7
Dean Court	F7
Dean Lane	G6
Dean Road	G5
Dean Street	F6
Dean Terrace	G5
Dean View	K4
Deanhill Lane	G5
Dee Avenue	H12
Denholm Way	G11
Derwent Court	F6
Derwent House	F7
Deveron Road	G11
Dick Road	G8
Ditton Drive	E12
Donaldson Drive	K5
Donaldson Road	K5
Doon Place	H12
Douglas Street	F9
Drumclog Place	H5

continued from page 55..

.		Bridgehousehill Road	F14	Burra Drive	G2
Bluebell Drive	E5	Bringan Road	F3	Burray Drive	G2
Bonnyton Place	D7	Brodick Road	C6	Busbiehill Place	D7
Bonnyton Road	C6, D7	Brodie Place	J6	Bussiehead Cottages	A3
Bowmore Place	D5	Broom Place	H11	Cairngorm Road	H13
Bowmore Road	D5	Broomhill Quadrant	G12	Cairns Terrace	E7
Boyd Court	G7	Broomhill Road East	G12	Calder Place	G11
Boyd Street	G7	Broomhill Road West	F12	Caledonia Court	E7
Boydston Way	J2	Bruce Crescent	F12	Cambuskeith Drive	B8
Brackenhill Avenue	G3	Bruce Street	F12	Cameron Drive	J6
Braefoot	F8	Buchanan Place	G11	Campbell Place	F11
Braehead Court	G8	Bunting Place	J9	Campbell Street	F11
Braeside Street	G8	Burnfoot Place	E4	Campbeltown Drive	F5
Brailsford Crescent	C10	Burnpark Road	F13	Campsie Road	G13
Bressay Place	H3	Burns Avenue	G5	Caprington Avenue	E13, F13
Brewery Road	F9	Burns Crescent	H3	Caprington Gardens	E13
Bridge Lane	F8	Burns Precinct	F7	Cardhu Crescent	D4
Bridgehouse Court	G14	Burns Way	H3	Cardhu Gardens	D4
		Burnside Street	E10	Carmel Avenue	C6

Name	Ref	Name	Ref
mmond Place	K6	Glassock Road	F3
f Place	J5	Glebe Avenue	G8
mfries Drive	B9	Glebe Court	G8
mgoyne Road	G13	Glebe Road	G8
nbar Drive	J6	Glen Affric Place	C10
ncan Court	K4	Glen Afton Court	C10
ndas Walk	J6	Glen Clova Gardens	C10
ndonald Court	H2	Glen Farrar Way	C10
ndonald Place	E9	Glen Lyon Crescent	C10
ndonald Road	B10, E9	Glen Nevis Place	C10
ngavel Road	G12	Glen Orchy Place	C10
nlop Street	F7	Glen Ord Crescent	E5
nn Mews	C8	Glen Orrin Avenue	C10
nnett Avenue	H9	Glen Shiel Crescent	C10
nnottar Drive	B8	Glen Trool Walk	C9
nollie Gardens	H2	Glen Truim View	C10
noon Avenue	F5	Glenapp Quadrant	H9
nskey Road	H2	Glencairn Square	F9
nure Drive	H8	Glencraigs Drive	F3
nure Place	H2	Glenfield Gardens	F10
rlston Avenue	F13	Glenfield Place	F10
rn Place	H11	Glenkinchie Road	D5
ast Gargieston Avenue	D10	Glenlivet Place	H5
ast Netherton Street	F9	Graham Place	J6
ast Shaw Street	F9	Graham Walk	J6
ast Woodstock Court	E8	Graithnock Drive	F6
day Crescent	F2	Grampian Road	H13
den Place	H11	Grange Place	F8
derslie Crescent	F12	Grange Street	F8
llis Lane	E8	Grange Terrace	D7
llis Street	E8	Granger Road	E11
llisland Drive	J8	Grant Place	J6
lmbank Avenue	G8	Grassyards Road	H6, H7
lmbank Drive	G8	Green Street	F7
riskay Place	H3	Greenan Road	H8
rskine Place	J6	Greenholm Street	F10
sk Road	H12	Grougar Drive	H3
sson Place	G5	Grougar Gardens	H4
ttrick Crescent	F5	Grougar Road	K8
velyn Villas	G7	Guthrie Terrace	B9
ailford Place	H3	Haining Avenue	G11
air Isle Place	G2	Hareshaw Drive	G3
airlie Avenue	D9	Hareshaw Gardens	G3
airyhill Place	E10	Harperland Drive	D9
airyhill Road	E10	Harriet Road	G6
aransay Place	G3	Harris Place	H3
arm Road	E5	Hawthorn Square	D8
enwick Close	J2	Hazel Avenue	D9
erguson Gardens	B8	Heather Place	D9
ern Place	C9	Hestan Place	H3
etlar Drive	G2	High Church Lane (1)	F7
inch Place	J9	High Glencairn Street	F9
inlayson Drive	K5	High Street	G7
ir Place	C9	Highet Street	F6
leming Street	E11	Highfield Avenue	G5
lotta Place	F2	Hill Street	F6
orbes Place	J6	Hillhead Square	F5
orbes Walk	H6	Hillpark Drive	F6
oregate, The	F7	Holehouse Road	G8
oregate Square	F7	Holly Place	D7
orest Grove	H3	Hollybush Place	H2
orth Place	G11	Holmes Crescent	D9
owlds Street	F8	Holmes Farm Road	D10
raser Walk	J6	Holmes Park Avenue	D10
ullarton Court	E7	Holmes Park Crescent	D10
ullarton Street	E8	Holmes Park Gardens	D10
ulton's Lane	F7	Holmes Park View	D10
ailes Place	E12	Holmes Park Wynd	D10
ainford Place	F4	Holmes Road	D10
allion Walk	G9	Holmes Village	D10
algrigside Road	D9	Holmlands Place	D10
alston Place	H2	Holmlea Drive	E10
arden Street	F7	Holmlea Place	E10
ardrum Place	F4	Holmquarry Road	F10
arnock Road	G11	Howard Court	F8
arrier Place	D6	Howard Park Drive	E9
arry Place	G11	Howard Street	E8
arven Court	H9	Huntly Court	J5
ateside Place	F12	Huntly Place	J6
ibson Street	D7	Hurlford Road	F11, G11
illsburn Gardens	G6	Inchgotrick Road	E12
ilmour Street	F9	Inchmurrin Drive	G3
lasgow Road	G4, H3, J1	Ingram Place	G5

Name	Ref	Name	Ref
Inkerman Place	E7	Lismore Road	G3
Innellan Drive	F5	Lister Street	A7
Invercloy Place	E4	Little Bellsland Road	F10
Iona Place	G3	Livingstone Court	J5
Irvine Road	B7, D7	Loanfoot Avenue	D7
Islay Place	H3	Loanhead Street	G8
James Johnston Place	G5	Loch View	J6
James Little Street	F9	Lochgreen Place	E12
James Shaw Lane (2)	F7	Lochlea	B9
James Sym Crescent	E10	Lochlea Wynd	B9
Jasmine Road	C9	Lochmaben Wynd	H2
Jean Armour Drive	B9	Lochnagar Road	G12
Jeffrey Street	F11	Lochranza Court	H2
John Burtt Place	G5	Lomond Road	G12
John Dickie Street	F7	London Gate	G8
John Finnie Street	F8	London Road	G8, H8
John Kennedy Place	G5	Loreny Drive	E13, E14
John Walker Drive	D4, D5	Loudoun Avenue	G12
Jura Gardens	D5	Low Church Lane (3)	F8
Jura Road	G3	Low Glencairn Street	F10
Kaimshill Cottages	K10	Lowther Place	G12
Katrine Court	G11	Luce Avenue	G11
Kay Park Crescent	H7	Lugar Wynd	H2
Kay Park Grove	G6	MacAdam Place	J7
Kay Park Terrace	G7	MacAllister Place	J7
Keith Place	J6	MacAlpine Place	J6
Kelburn Crescent	E12	MacAndrew Place	J7
Ken Road	G11	MacAuley Place	J7
Kennedy Court	J5	MacBeth Drive	K7
Kennedy Drive	J5, K5	MacBeth Gardens	J7
Kennedy Street	F10	MacBeth Walk	J7
Kerr Road	K6	MacCallum Drive	J7
Kilmarnock Road	A7	MacCallum Place	J7
Kilmaurs Road	E4	MacDonald Drive	J7
Kilmory Place	E4	Macdonald Gardens	J7
King Street	F8	MacDonald Place	J7
Kingsford Place	H3	MacDougall Drive (1)	J7
Kingswell Avenue	G3	MacDougall Place	J7
Kinloch Road	G11	MacEwan Place	J8
Kinnoull Road	G13	MacFarlane Drive	J7
Kirkton Road	F3	MacGregor Drive	H8
Kirktonholm Place	F9	MacNichol Gardens	J7
Kirktonholm Street	F8	MacNichol Place	J7
Kirkwall Place	G3	MacInnes Place	J7
Knockando Place	D5	MacIntosh Place	J7
Knockinlaw Mount	F4	MacIntyre Place	J7
Knockinlaw Road	F4	MacIvor Place	J7
Knockmarloch Drive	F13	MacKellar Place	J6
Knowehead Road	F12	MacKendrick Place	J8
Laburnum Road	C9	MacKenzie Drive	H7
Lagavulin Place	E5	MacKinlay Place	G9
Lainshaw Avenue	E13	MacKinnon Drive	J8
Lamlash Gardens	G4	MacLaren Place	J8
Lammermuir Road	G13	MacLean Drive	H7
Landsborough Drive	G5	MacLeod Drive	J8
Langcraig Road	F14	MacLeod Place	J8
Langlands Brae	F7	MacMillan Drive (2)	J7
Langlands Street	F7	MacMillan Place	J7
Langside Avenue	F13	MacNab Place	H7
Laputa Place	E13	MacNaughton Drive	J7
Larch Place	D8	MacNaughton Walk	J6
Largs Avenue	H5	MacNeil Place	H7
Lauder Court	J5	MacPhail Drive	J7
Laurel Place	D9	MacPherson Gardens	J7
Lauriston Way	H2	MacPherson Place	J7
Lawers Crescent	G12	MacPherson Walk	J7
Lawers Road	G12	McIlvanney Crescent	F6
Lawson Street	G9	McIlvanney Drive	F6
Leadhills Road	G13	McLelland Drive	E9
Lennox Crescent	D7	Machrie Road	E4
Lerwick Place	G2	Mackie Place	J7
Leslie Place	H6	Main Road	K9
Leslie Road	H6	Manor Avenue	G4
Leven Avenue	G5	Manse Street	G8
Lewis Drive	H3	Maple Place	D8
Lilac Place	E8	Marchdyke Crescent	E13
Lime Place	D8	Mathew Smith Avenue	E10
Lindsay Drive	J5	MauchlIne Court	H2
Lindsay Street	E8	Maxholm Road	E11
Linfern Avenue	J8		
Linfern Avenue East	J9		
Linfern Avenue West	J9	*continued overleaf...*	

continued overleaf...

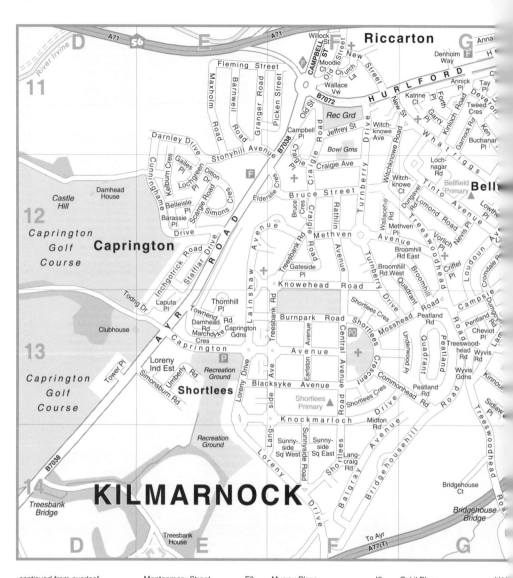

continued from overleaf...

Maxwell Court	K5	Montgomery Street	F6
Meiklewood Road	F4	Moodie Court	F11
Melville Street	H8	Moorfield Avenue	D10
Merrick Road	H12	Morris Lane	G7
Methven Avenue	F12	Morrison Place	J6
Methven Place	F12	Morton Place	F7
Mews Lane	E9	Morven Avenue	F4, F5
Middlemass Drive	H8	Mossgiel Avenue	J8
Midton Road	F13	Mosshead Road	F13
Mill Court	G9	Mosside Place	F4
Mill Street	F9	Mount Avenue	D10
Millhill Terrace	E4	Mount House	B9
Milton Avenue	J7	Mount Place	D10
Milton Drive	J7	Mount Pleasant Way	F7
Milton Road	J8	Mount Village	C9
Mitchell Court	G8	Muirend Road	F3
Montgomery Place	F6	Munro Avenue	D7
		Munro Place	E6
		Mure Avenue	G4

Murray Place	J6	Ochil Place	H13
Nelson Street	F8	Ochiltree Place	H2
Nevis Place	G12	Ogilvie Place	J6
New Mill Road	G9	Old Irvine Road	E8
New Street	F11	Old Mill Road	G8
Newlands Drive	E4	Old Rome Drive	B9
Newlands Place	E4	Old Street	F10, F11
Newmilns Gardens	H2	Oliphant Drive	J8
Newton Walk	G9	Olive Road	D8
Nith Place	H10	Onthank Drive	E4
Niven Court	K4	Orchard Gardens	F6
North Gargieston Road	C10	Orchard Street	F6
North Hamilton Place	E7	Orkney Drive	G3
North Hamilton Street	E8	Osprey Drive	J9
Nursery Avenue	G8	Otterburn Avenue	H5
Nursery Gardens	H9	Park Lane	F7
Nursery Lane	H8	Park Street	E7
Nursery Street	F9	Park View	G6
Oak Place	D8	Paxton Place	G9

Queen's Drive	G10	Springhill Stables	E8	Wellington Avenue	K8
Raasay Place	G2	Springhill View	E8	Wellington Place	F6
Raithburn Avenue	F4	Square of Ales	F7	Wellington Street	F7
Ralston Drive	K8	Stafflar Drive	E12	Wellpark Avenue	J8
Rankin Court	J5	Stafford Street	F6	Wellpark Court	J8
Rathlin Avenue	F12	Station Drive	K10	Wellpark Grove	J8
Redding Avenue	F4	Stevenson Court	D7	Wellpark Place	J8
Rennie Street	F8	Stevenson Street	D7	West Fullarton Street	E7
Riccarton Road	J10	Stewarton Crescent	H2	West George Street	F7
Richardland Place	G9	Stirling Avenue	C7	West Langlands Street	E7
Richardland Road (6)	F9	Stirling Crescent	C7	West Netherton Street	F9
Ritchie Court	J6	Stonyhill Avenue	E11	West Shaw Street	F9
Riverbank Place	G9	Stornoway Drive	G2	West Woodstock Court	E8
Robert Creighton Place	F7	Strand Street	F7	West Woodstock Street	E8
Robert Noble Place	D6	Strawberrybank Road	G6	Western Place	G4
Robert Stewart Place	E7	Stronsay Place	G3	Western Road	F5, G4
Robertson Place	G8	Struthers Avenue	K8	Westfield Road	J2
Rona Place	H3	Sturrock Street	F8	Westmoor Crescent	D9
Rosebank Place	F6	Sunnyside Road	F14	Westray Drive	G2
Ross Walk	H6	Sunnyside Square East	F14	Whatriggs Road	G11
Rothesay Place	F5	Sunnyside Square West	F14	William Street	F6
Rousay Wynd	G2	Sutherland Drive	K7	Willie Mairs Brae	G6
Rowallan Drive	G4	Swallow Place	J9	Willie Ross Place	K4
Rowan Place	D9	Talisker Avenue	D4	Willock Street	F11
Rowanhill Place	D9	Talisker Gardens	E4	Willow Road	D8
Rugby Crescent	D9	Talisker Rigg	D4	Wilson Avenue	G8
Rugby Road	D9	Tannock Street	F10	Witch Road	F6
Rumford Place	J2	Tarbolton Place	J2	Witchill Place	F6
Russell Court	J5	Tay Place	G11	Witchknowe Avenue	F11
St Andrew's Court (5)	F8	Teith Place	H11	Witchknowe Court	F12
St Andrew's Street	F8	Thirdpart Place	D9	Witchknowe Road	F12
St Andrews Street	F9	Thomas Baird Gardens	F5	Woodhill Road	E5
St Andrew's Walk	F9	Thomson Street	F6	Woodlands Grove	H4
St Marnock Place (4)	F8	Thorn Terrace	G4	Woodlands Place	G4
St Marnock Street	F8	Thornhill Place	E13	Woodside Avenue	D10
St Maur's Crescent	E5	Tinto Avenue	G12	Woodstock Place	E7
St Maur's Place	E5	Titchfield Street	F9	Woodstock Street	E8
St Michael's Mount	B9	Titwood Drive	F4	Wyvis Gardens	G13
Samson Avenue	H8	Tobermory Drive	D5	Wyvis Road	G13
Sanda Place	G3	Todhill Avenue	F4	Yorke Place	D7
Sandbed Lane	F8	Todrig Drive	E13		
Sandbed Street	F8	Toponthank Lane	G2		
Sannox Road	C6	Tourhill Road	E4		
Scalpay Place	G3	Tower Place	D13		
Scargie Road	E12	Townend Road	E13		
Scott Crescent	E9	Townhead Gardens	G6		
Scott Road	E9, E10	Townholm	G6		
Seaford Street	E8	Treesbank Road	F12, F13		
Seright Crescent	K9	Treeswoodhead	G12, G13		
Seright Square	K8	Road			
Shanks Court	F6	Trondra Gardens	G2		
Shanter Place	J8	Turnberry Drive	F12		
Shawbank Place	G9	Turner Place	G5		
Shetland Drive	G2	Tweed Crescent	G11		
Shiskine Drive	E4	Uist Lane	G2		
Shortlees Crescent	F13	Umberly Road	E13		
Shortlees Road	F14	Underwood Place	G13		
Sidlaw Place	G13	Union Street	F7		
Silverwood Road	K8	Urquhart Road	K6		
Simons Crescent	E12	Vatersay Place	G2		
Simonsburn Road	E13	Victoria East Road	G9		
Simpson Street	A7	Victoria Terrace	G9		
Sinclair Court	J5	Vorlich Place	G12		
Skene Road	J5	Vrackie Place	G12		
Skye Gardens	G2	Waddell Court	F4		
Smiddy Court	F10	Walker Avenue	H8		
Smillie Place	C10	Wallace Street	E9		
Solway Place	H12	Wallace View	F11		
Soulis Street	F7	Wallacehill Road	F12		
Souter Drive	J8	Wallacetown Avenue	H2		
South Dean Road	G6	Walnut Road	C9		
South Gargieston Drive	C10	Wardneuk Drive	G4		
South Hamilton Court	E8	Wards Place	F9		
South Hamilton Place	E9	Warwickhill Place	E6		
South Hamilton Street	E9	Warwickhill Road	D7		
Southcraig Avenue	J2	Water Lane	F8		
Southcraig Drive	G2	Waterside Court	F8		
Southhook Road	D6	Waterside Street	F8		
Sparrow Gardens	J9	Watson Street	H8		
Spey Avenue	G11	Waulkmill Place	G9		
Springhill Gardens	E8	Waverley Avenue	C7		
Springhill Place	E8	Welbeck Street	G9		

...ace Avenue	D7
...eatland Quadrant	G13
...eatland Road	G13
...entland Road	G13
...cken Street	F11
...ne Road	D9
...orter Drive	B10
...orting Cross Place	H2
...ortland Place	E8
...ortland Road	E8
...ortland Street	F7
...ortree Avenue	G2
...otteries, The	D6
...ottery Place	F6
...riestland Close	H2
...rimrose Place	D7
...rinces Street	F8
...rincess Court	H12
...Queen Street	F8

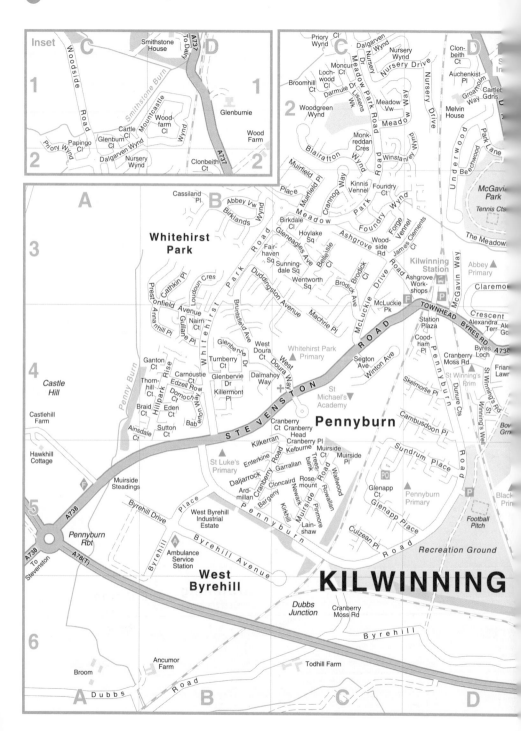

Inset

Woodside Road

Smithstone House

To Dalry

Glenburnie

Woodfarm Cl

Mountcastle Wynd

Smithstone Burn

Wood Farm

Cartle Cl

Glenburn Cl

Priory Wynd

Papingo Cl

Dalgarven Wynd

Nursery Wynd

Clonbeith Ct

Priory Wynd

Dalgarven Wynd

Nursery Wynd

Clonbeith Ct

Auchenkist Pl

Groatholm Way

Cartlebridge Gdns

Moncur Ct

Meadow Park Road

Nursery Drive

Nursery Drive

Broomhill Ct

Lochwood Cl

Darmule Cl

Lissens Wk

Meadow Vw

Meadow Way

Melvin House

Woodgreen Wynd

Monkreddan Cres

Meadow Wynd

Meadow

Underwood

Park Lane

Beechwood

McGavin Park

Tennis Cts

Blairafton

Muirfield Pl

Muirfield Place

Crannog Way

Kinnis Vennel

Foundry Ct

Park Road

The Meadow

Cassiland Pl

Abbey Vw

Birklands

Meadow

Birkdale Cl

Foundry Wynd

Forge Vennel

James Clements Cl

Whitehirst Park

Wynd

Hoylake Sq

Gleneagles Ave

Belisle

Ashgrove Rd

Woodside Rd

Kilwinning Station

Ashgrove Workshops

Abbey Primary

Claremo

Park Road

Fairhaven Sq

Sunningdale Sq

Wentworth Sq

Brodick Cl

Brodick Ave

McLuckie Pk

McGavin Way

Crescent

Cathkin Pl

Prestonfield Avenue

Loudoun Cres

Duddingston Avenue

Machrie Pl

McLuckie Drive

Station Plaza

Alexandra Terr

Byres Loch

A738

Anna hill Pl

Nairn Ct

Gullane Pl

Bruntsfield Ave

West Doura Ct

Whitehirst Park Primary

Segton Ave

Coodham Pl

Cranberry Moss Rd

Friars Lawr

Ganton Ct

Glenbervie Dr

Turnberry Ct

West Doura Way

Winton Ave

Skelmorlie Pl

St Winning's Prim

St Winning's Rd

Thornhill Ct

Carnoustie Ct

Glenbervie Dr

Dalmahoy Way

St Michael's Academy

Dunure Cts

Pennyburn

Castle Hill

Edzell Row

Kyle Crt

Killermont Pl

St Luke's Primary

Cambusdoon Pl

Hillpark Ct

Domoch Ct

Eden Ct

Bab

Cranberry Ct

Cranberry Head

Sundrum Place

Castlehill Farm

Braid Ct

Ainsdale Ct

Sutton Ct

Kilkerran

Kelburne

Cranberry Pl

Muirside Ct

Muirside Pl

Glenapp Ct

Hawkhill Cottage

Enterkine

Daljarrock

Cranberry Road

Garrallan

Trees- bank

Wallwood

Pennyburn Primary

Black Prim

Muirside Steadings

Ardmillan

Cloncaird

Rosemount

Rowallan

Glenapp Place

Football Pitch

STEVENSTON ROAD

Byrehill Drive

Place

West Byrehill Industrial Estate

Bargeny

Newark

Pinmore

Kirkhill

Lainshaw

Culzean Pl

Road

Recreation Ground

Byrehill

Pennyburn Rbt

A738

A78(T)

To Stevenston

Ambulance Service Station

West Byrehill

Byrehill Avenue

KILWINNING

Dubbs Junction

Cranberry Moss Rd

Byrehill

Broom

Ancumor Farm

Todhill Farm

Dubbs Road

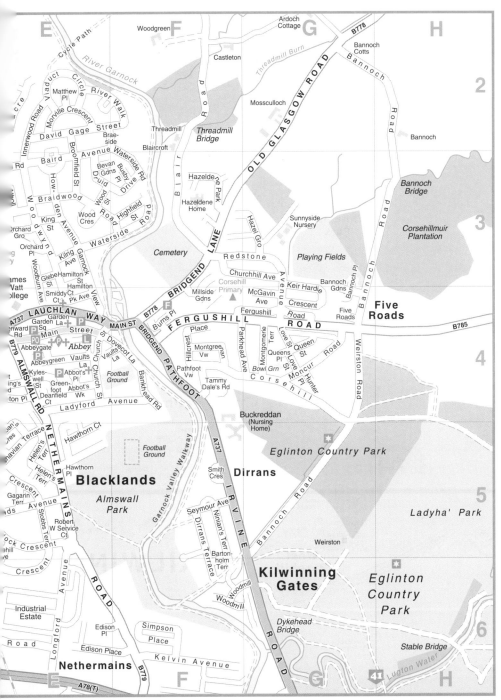

Index to street names can be found starting on page 98

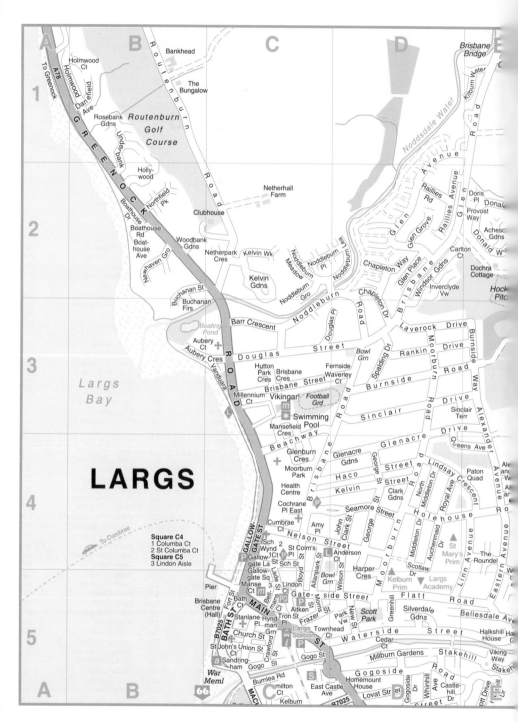

Square C4
1 Columba Ct
2 St Columba Ct
Square C5
3 Lindon Aisle

LARGS

Largs Bay

Routenburn Golf Course

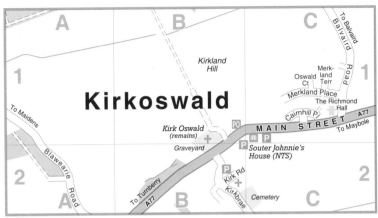

Kirkoswald

Kirkland Hill

Merkland Ct
Oswald Terr

Merkland Place
The Richmond Hall

Cairnhill P.

MAIN STREET
To Maybole

Kirk Oswald
(remains)

Graveyard

Souter Johnnie's
House (NTS)

Kirk Rd

Cemetery

To Maidens

To Turnberry
A77

Blawearie Road

A77

To Balvaird
Balvaird Road

Index to Kirkoswald

Balvaird Road	C1
Blawearie Road	A2
Cairnhill Place	C1
Kirk Road	B2
Kirkbrae	B2
Oswald Court	C1
Main Street	C1
Merkland Place	C1
Merkland Terrace	C1

Index to Largs

Acheson Gardens	E2	Brisbane Road	C4
Acre Avenue	D7	Brisbane Street	C3
Aitken Street	C5	Broom Court	D6
Alexander Avenue	E3	Broomfield Crescent	C6
Alexander Court	E4	Broomfield Place	C6
Alexander Walk	E4	Broomfield	C6
Allanpark Street	C4	Buchanan Firs	B3
Amy Place	C4	Buchanan Street	B2
Anderson Court	D4	Burnlea Road	C5
Anthony Court	C4	Burnside Road	D3
Anthony Road	D7	Burnside Way	E3
Arran View	E4	Carlton Court	E2
Aubery Court	B3	Castle Bay Court	C6
Aubery Crescent	B3	Castlehill Drive	D5
Auchenmaid Drive	D4	Cathcart Road	D6
Bankhouse Avenue	D6	Cedar Court	D5
Bankhouse Crescent	D6	Chapelton Drive	D2
Bankhouse Grove	E6	Chapelton Way	D2
Barr Crescent	C3	Charles Street	C6
Bath Court	C5	Church Street	C5
Bath Street	C5	Clark Gardens	D4
Beachway	C4	Cochrane Place East	C4
Bellesdale Avenue	E5	Columba Court (1)	C4
Bellmans Close	C5	Court Street	C4
Blackdales Avenue	D6	Crawford Street	C5
Blythswood Crescent	D6	Cumbrae Court	C4
Boathouse Avenue	B2	Cunningham Drive	D6
Boathouse Drive	B2	Curlinghall	D6
Boathouse Road	B2	Dalry Road	E7
Bowen Craig Walk	D8	Danefield Avenue	D6
Bowen Craig	D7	Donald Wynd	E2
Boyd Street	C4	Doris Place	E2
Braeside Avenue	E4	Douglas Place	C3
Brisbane Crescent	C3	Douglas Street	C3
Brisbane Glen Road	D3	Duffield Drive	D7
		East Castle Avenue	C5
		Eastern Avenue	E5
		Elderslie Gardens	C6
		Fernside	D3
		Flatt Road	D5
		Fort Street	C5
		Frazer Street	C5
		Gallowgate Lane	C4
		Gallowgate Square	C4
		Gallowgate Street	C4
		Gateside Street	C5
		George Street	D4
		Glen Avenue	D2
		Glen Grove	D2
		Glen Place	D2
		Glenacre Drive	D4
		Glenacre Gardens	D4
		Glenburn Crescent	C4
		Gogo Street	C5
		Gogoside Drive	D5
		Gogoside Road	D5
		Greenhill	D5
		Greenock Road	B1
		Greeto Falls Avenue	E4
		Haco Street	D4
		Halkshill Drive	E5
		Halkshill Gardens	E5
		Halkshill House	E5
		Hamilton Court	C5
		Hamilton Drive	D6
		Harper Crescent	D4
		Haylie Brae	E7
		Haylie Gardens	D6
		Haylie Neuk	D6
		Hill Street	C6
		Holehouse Court	E4
		Holehouse Road	D4
		Hollywood	B2
		Holmwood Court	B1
		Holmwood	A1
		Homemount House	D5
		Hutcheson Drive	D7
		Hutton Park Crescent	C3
		Hyndman Green	C5
		Inverclyde View	D2
		Irvine Road	D5, E8
		John Clark Street	D4
		John Street	C6
		Kelburn Court	C6
		Kelvin Gardens	C2
		Kelvin Street	D4
		Kelvin Walk	C2
		Kilburn Water	E1
		Kyles View	E4
		Lade Street	C5
		Laverock Drive	D3
		Lindsay Crescent	D4
		Lindon Aisle (3)	C5
		Lindon Court	C5
		Linn Avenue	E4
		Lovat Street	D5
		Mackerston Place	C6

continued overleaf...

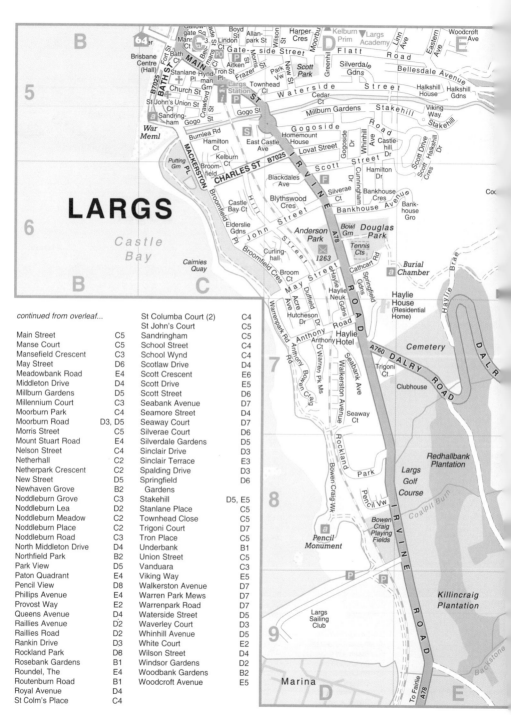

LARGS

continued from overleaf...

Main Street	C5	St Columba Court (2)	C4
Manse Court	C5	St John's Court	C5
Mansefield Crescent	C3	Sandringham	C5
May Street	D6	School Street	C4
Meadowbank Road	E4	School Wynd	C4
Middleton Drive	D4	Scotlaw Drive	D4
Millburn Gardens	D5	Scott Crescent	E6
Millennium Court	C3	Scott Drive	E5
Moorburn Park	C4	Scott Street	D6
Moorburn Road	D3, D5	Seabank Avenue	D7
Morris Street	C5	Seamore Street	D4
Mount Stuart Road	E4	Seaway Court	D7
Nelson Street	C4	Silverae Court	D6
Netherhall	C2	Silverdale Gardens	D5
Netherpark Crescent	C2	Sinclair Drive	D3
New Street	D5	Sinclair Terrace	E3
Newhaven Grove	B2	Spalding Drive	D3
Noddleburn Grove	C3	Springfield	D6
Noddleburn Lea	D2	Gardens	
Noddleburn Meadow	C2	Stakehill	D5, E5
Noddleburn Place	C2	Stanlane Place	C5
Noddleburn Road	C3	Townhead Close	C5
North Middleton Drive	D4	Trigoni Court	D7
Northfield Park	B2	Tron Place	C5
Park View	D5	Underbank	B1
Paton Quadrant	E4	Union Street	C5
Pencil View	D8	Vanduara	C3
Phillips Avenue	E4	Viking Way	E5
Provost Way	E2	Walkerston Avenue	D7
Queens Avenue	D4	Warren Park Mews	D7
Raillies Avenue	D2	Warrenpark Road	D7
Raillies Road	D2	Waterside Street	D5
Rankin Drive	D3	Waverley Court	D3
Rockland Park	D8	Whinhill Avenue	D5
Rosebank Gardens	B1	White Court	E2
Roundel, The	E4	Wilson Street	D4
Routenburn Road	B1	Windsor Gardens	D2
Royal Avenue	D4	Woodbank Gardens	B2
St Colm's Place	C4	Woodcroft Avenue	E5

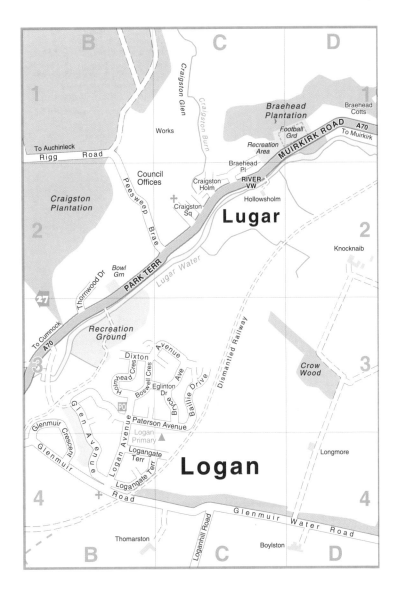

Index to Logan & Lugar

Baillie Drive	C3	Eglinton Drive	C3	Loganhill Road	C4
Boswell Crescent	B3	Glen Avenue	B3	Muirkirk Road	C1
Braehead Cottages	D1	Glenmuir Crescent	B3	Park Terrace	B2
Braehead Place	C2	Glenmuir Road	B4	Paterson Avenue	B3
Bryce Avenue	C3	Glenmuir Water Road	D4	Peesweep Brae	B2
Craigston Holm	C2	Holmhead Crescent	B3	Rigg Road	B1
Craigston Square	C2	Logan Avenue	B4	River View	C2
Dixton Avenue	B3	Logangate Terrace	B4	Thornwood Drive	B2

Mauchline

Inset

Smithy

CATRINE ROAD

Sawmill Cottage

Clubhouse

Ball

East Mossgiel

Robert Burns Memorial Stone

Tarbolton Road

KILMARNOCK ROAD

A76

To Kilmarnock

Jean Armour Burns Houses

Bowl Grn

Burns Memorial Cotts

Works

Hillhead Road

West Hillhead

National Burns Memorial

Laurland

Sunnyside Road

Lindsay Ct

Jean Armour Drive

Hughfield Rd

Beechwood Road

Carrick View

Jean Armour Crescent

Wee Wood

Burns Ave

Campbell Ave

Ellisland Ct

Mauchline Mains

Mauchline Burn

Jean Armour Dr

Loch Rd

Nursery La

Mauchline Primary

Community Centre

Nether Pl

Nether Pl Gdns

Burn-side Rd

Knowe

Castle St

Green-head

Burngrange La

Kemp Ct

Loan Green

B743

Mansfield Rd

Robert Burns Pl

HIGH ST

LOAN

Welton

Bus Depot

Loanhill Ave

Mossgiel Avenue

Mary Mo

THE CROSS

Horwood Pl

Cow-gate

Curling Stone Pl

Grove Pk

EARL GREY ST

Glebe Ave

Ballochmyl Ave

Roa

Bogwood

NEW RD

South Park Ave

East Park Ave

Clarinda Cres

Nether Wall

Tanfield

Rankin Dr

Bowl Grn

Lochlea Ave

Gregory St

So fie A

Nether Pl

West-side Gdns

Clelland Park

West Park Ave

Barskimming Rd

Beechgrove Rd

Playing Field

Donaldson Cres

B705

CATRI

Temple Bogwood Bridge

AYR ROAD

5.5m

Arran View

Connel Crescent

Rawson Cres

Whiteford Pl

Corrie Mains Farm

Grassmillees Holdings

Burnisland Cres

Grassmillees Way

South Lodge

B743

To Mossblown

Connel Crescent

Pollocks Way

Station La

Station Road Ind Est

Victoria Cotts

CUMNOCK ROA

Gateside

Southfield Kennels

Mosshead Smallholdings

Barskimming Road

Cemetery

Haugh Road

Sawmill

Glendale Cottage

Mosshead Nos 1 & 2

Quarry (disused)

Woodlands No 3

Haughyett

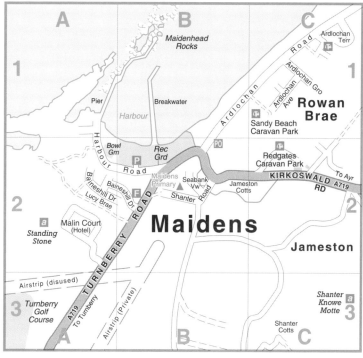

Maidens

Index to Mauchline

Alexander Terrace	D3
Anderson Avenue	E4
Arran View	B4
Auld Avenue	D3
Ayr Road	B4
Ballochmyle Avenue	D3
Ballochmyle Way	G5
Barskimming Road	B5, C4
Beechgrove Road	C4
Beechwood Road	B2
Burngrange Lane	C3
Burns Avenue	C2
Burns Memorial Cottages	B1
Burnside Road	C3
Burnsland Crescent	D4
Campbell Avenue	C2
Carrick View	B2
Castle Street	C3
Catrine Road	D4, F5
Clarinda Crescent	C3
Clelland Park	C4
Connel Crescent	B4
Cowgate	C3
Cross, The	C3
Cumnock Road	D4
Curling Stone Place	C3
Donaldson Crescent	D4
Earl Grey Street	C3
East Park Avenue	C4
Ellisland Court	C2
Fernlea Avenue	D4
Glebe Avenue	C3, D3
Grassmillees Way	D4
Greenhead	C3
Gregory Street	D4
Grove Park	C3
Hamilton Avenue	D4
Haugh Road	C5
High Street	C3
Hillhead Road	B1
Horwood Place	C3
Howford	G5
Hughfield Road	C2
Jean Armour Burns Houses	B1
Jean Armour Drive	C2
Kemp Court	C3
Kilmarnock Road	B1
Knowe	C3
Lindsay Court	C2
Loan	D3
Loanhill Avenue	D3
Loch Road	C2
Lochlea Avenue	D4
Loudoun Street	C3
Mansfield Road	C3
Mary Morrison Drive	D3
Mossgiel Avenue	D3
Nether Place	C3, B3
Nether Place Gardens	C3
Nether Walk	C3
New Road	C3
Nursery Lane	C2
Pollocks Way	C4
Rankin Drive	D3
Rawson Crescent	B4
Robert Burns Place	C3
Sorn Road	D3
South Park Avenue	B3
Southfield Avenue	D4
Station Lane	C4
Station Road	C4
Sunnyside Crescent	C2
Tanfield	C3
Tarbolton Road	A1
Victoria Cottages	C4
Welton Road	D3
West Park Avenue	C4
Westgate	F5
Westside Gardens	B4
Whiteford Place	B4

Index to Maidens

Ardlochan Avenue	C1
Ardlochan Grove	C1
Ardlochan Road	B1
Ardlochan Terrace	C1
Baineshill Drive	A2
Harbour Road	A1
Jameston Cottages	B2
Kirkoswald Road	C2
Lucy Brae	A2
Seabank View	B2
Shanter Cottages	C3
Shanter Road	B2
Turnberry Road	A3

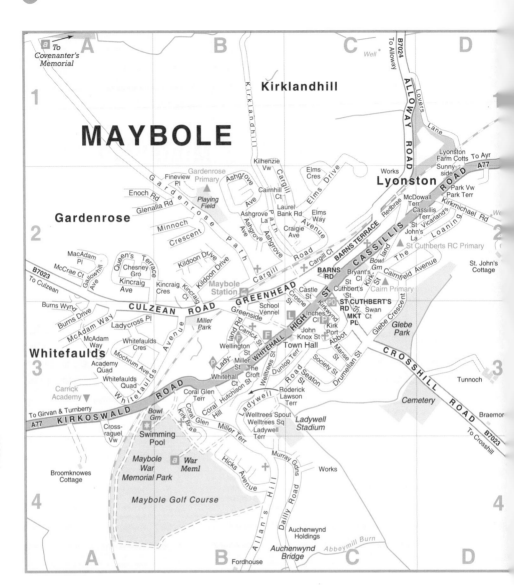

a To Covenanter's Memorial

MAYBOLE

Kirklandhill

To Alloway

Well

Lyonston

Lyonston Farm Cotts To Ayr
Sunnyside
A77

Works

Park Vw
Park Terr

McDowall Terr

Kirkmichael Rd

Cassillis Terr

St Vicarland

Kilhenzie Vw

Elms Cres

Fineview Pl

Gardenrose Primary

Ashgrove Ave

Cairnhill Ct

Elms Drive

Enoch Rd

Playing Field

Laurel Bank Rd

Elms Way

Gardenrose

Glenalla Rd

Ashgrove La

Craigie Ave

Ashgrove Ave

Ashgrove Ave

Avenue

St John's La

St Cuthberts RC Primary

Minnoch

Crescent

Cargill Road

Barns Terrace

Cassillis

Redrae

The Loaning

St. John's Cottage

MacAdam Pl

Queen's Terrace

Kildoon Drive

Cargill Ct

BARNS RD

Bowl Gm

Cairnfield Avenue

McCrae Ct

Chesney Gro

Kildoon Drive

Cargill

Castle St

Bryant's St Cl

St Cuthbert's St

Cairn Primary

B7023
To Culzean

Gallowhill Ave

Kincraig Ave

Kincraig Cres

Kincraig Ct

Maybole Station

GREENHEAD

HIGH ST

ST CUTHBERT'S RD

Glebe Crescent

Glebe Park

Burns Wynd

Burns Drive

CULZEAN ROAD

Greenside

School Vennel

Crosne

Kirkwynd

MKT PL

Swan

L

Inches Cl

PO

McAdam Way

Ladycross Pl

Miller Park

Carrick Pl

John Knox St

Kirk Port Abbot

Manse St

McAdam Way

Whitefaulds Cres

Wellington St

WHITEHALL

Town Hall

Whitefaulds

Mochrum Ave

Miller St

Society St

Drumellan St

CROSSHILL ROAD

Tunnoch

Academy Quad

Whitefaulds Quad

P

Lady St

The Croft

Dunlop Terr

Road Seaton

Carrick Academy ▼

WHITEFAULDS ROAD

KIRKOSWALD ROAD

Whitehall Ct

Roderick Lawson Terr

Cemetery

To Girvan & Turnberry
A77

Coral Glen Terr

Coral Glen Hill

Hutchison Hill

Ladywell

Welltrees Spout

Braemor

B7023
To Crosshill

Broomknowes Cottage

Crossraguel Vw

Bowl Grn

Coral Glen Brae

Kirk Brae

Miller Terr

Welltrees Sq

Ladywell Terr

Ladywell Stadium

Swimming Pool

a War Meml

Hicks Avenue

Murray Gdns

Works

Maybole War Memorial Park

Maybole Golf Course

Allans Hill

Dailly Road

Auchenwynd Holdings

Auchenwynd Bridge

Abbeymill Burn

Fordhouse

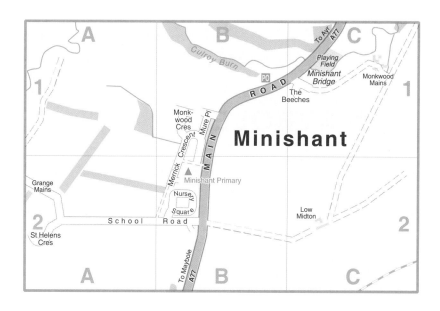

Minishant

Index to Maybole

Abbot Street	C3
Academy Quadrant	A3
Allan's Hill	B4
Alloway Road	C1
Ashgrove	B2
Ashgrove Avenue	B2
Ashgrove Lane	B2
Barns Road	C2
Barns Terrace	C2
Bryant's Close	C2
Burns Drive	A3
Burns Wynd	A3
Cairnfield Avenue	C2
Cairnhill Court	B2
Cargill Avenue	C2
Cargill Court	C2
Cargill Road	B2
Carrick Street	B3
Cassillis Road	C2
Cassillis Terrace	D2
Castle Street	C2
Chesney Grove	A2
Coral Glen	B3
Coral Glen Terrace	B3
Coral Hill	B3
Craigie Avenue	C2
Croft, The	B3
Crosne Street	C2
Crosshill Road	D3
Crossraguel View	A3
Culzean Road	B3
Dailly Road	C4
Drumellan Street	C3
Dunlop Terrace	B3
Elms Crescent	C2
Elms Drive	C2
Elms Way	C2
Enoch Road	A2
Fineview Place	B2
Gallowhill Avenue	A2
Gardenrose Path	B2
Glebe Crescent	C3
Glenalla Road	A2
Greenhead	B3
Greenside	B3
Hicks Avenue	B4
High Street	C3
Hutchison Street	B3
Inches Close	C3
John Knox Street	C3
Kildoon Drive	B2
Kilhenzie View	B1
Kincraig Avenue	A2
Kincraig Court	B2
Kincraig Crescent	B2
Kirk Brae	B3
Kirk Port	C3
Kirkland Street	C2
Kirklandhill Path	B1
Kirkmichael Road	D2
Kirkoswald Road	A3
Kirkwynd	C3
Ladycross Place	A3
Ladyland Road	B3
Ladywell Road	B3
Ladywell Terrace	B3
Laurel Bank Road	B2
Loaning, The	D2
Lovers Lane	D1
Lyonston Farm Cottages	D1
MacAdam Place	A2
McAdam Way	A3
McCrae Court	A2
McDowall Terrace	D2
Manse Street	C3
Market Place	C3
Miller Street	B3
Miller Terrace	B3
Minnoch Crescent	B2
Mochrum Avenue	A3
Murray Gardens	C4
Park Terrace	D2
Park View	D2
Queen's Terrace	A2
Redbrae	C2
Roderick Lawson Terrace	B3
St Cuthberts Road	C3
St Cuthberts Street	C2
St John's Lane	D2
School Vennel	B3
Seaton Street	C3
Society Street	C3
Sunnyside	D2
Swan Court	C3
Vicarlands	D2
Wellington Street	B3
Welltrees Spout	B3
Welltrees Square	B3
Welltrees Street	B3
Whitefaulds Avenue	A3
Whitefaulds Crescent	A3
Whitefaulds Quadrant	A3
Whitehall	B3
Whitehall Court	B3

Index to Minishant

Beeches, The	C1
Merrick Crescent	B2
Monkwood Crescent	B1
Mure Place	B1
Nursery Square	B2
St Helens Crescent	A2
School Road	A2

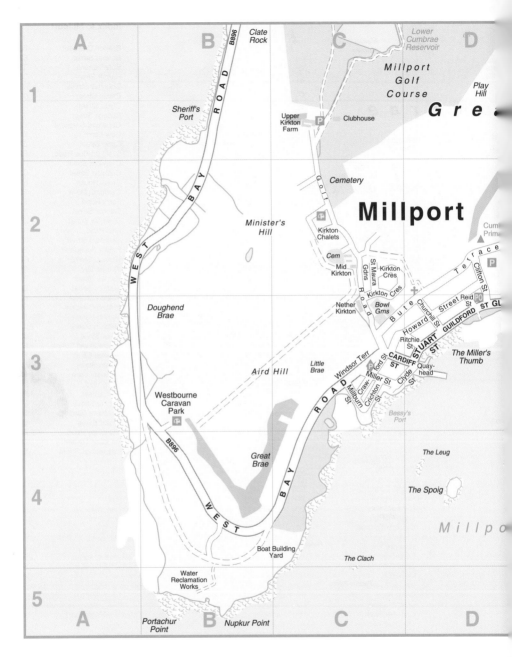

Clate Rock

Lower Cumbrae Reservoir

Millport Golf Course

Play Hill

Sheriff's Port

Upper Kirkton Farm

Clubhouse

Gre

Cemetery

Millport

Minister's Hill

Kirkton Chalets

Cum Prima

Cem

St Maura Gdns

Kirkton Cres

Mid Kirkton

Kirkton Cres

Terrace

Clifton St

Doughend Brae

Nether Kirkton

Kirkton Road

Bute Road

Churchill St

Howard Street

Reid St

ST GL

Bowl Grns

Guildford ST

Aird Hill

Little Brae

Windsor Terr

Ritchie St

Stuart ST

The Miller's Thumb

Westbourne Caravan Park

Great Brae

Milburn St

Craw-ford St

Crichton St

Miller St

Clyde St

Cardiff ST

Quay-head

Bessy's Port

The Leug

The Spoig

B896

WEST BAY ROAD

Boat Building Yard

The Clach

Millpo

Water Reclamation Works

Portachur Point

Nupkur Point

A   B   C   D

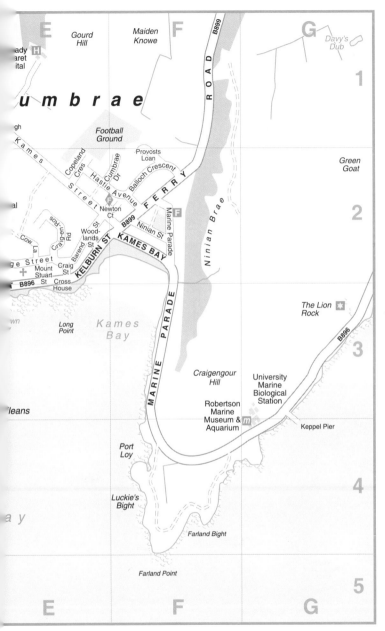

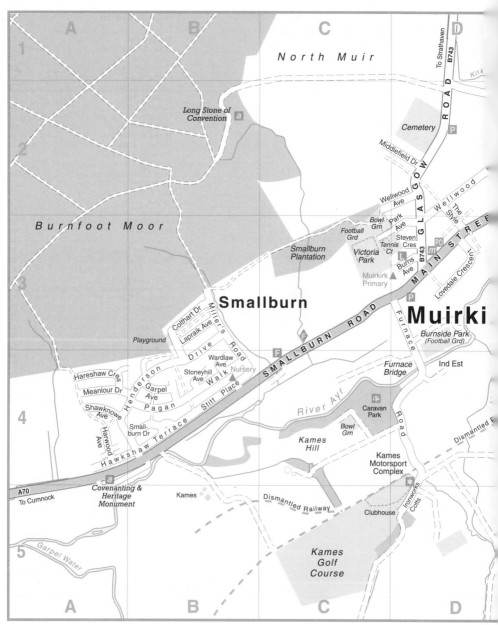

North Muir

To Strathaven

B743

Kitk

Long Stone of Convention

Cemetery

Middlefield Dr

GLASGOW ROAD

Wellwood Ave

Wellwood

The Style

Burnfoot Moor

Bowl Grn

Park Ave

Football Grd

Steven Cres

Smallburn Plantation

Tennis Ct

Victoria Park

MAIN STREE

PO

Muirkirk Primary

Burns Ave

B743

Lovedale Crescent

Smallburn

Muirki

Colthart Dr

Lapraik Ave

Miller's Road

SMALLBURN ROAD

Furnace

Burnside Park
(Football Grd)

Playground

Drive

Wardlaw Ave

Furnace Bridge

Ind Est

Henderson

Stoneyhill Ave

Nursery

Walk

Hareshaw Cres

Garpel Ave

Stitt Place

River Ayr

Caravan Park

Meanlour Dr

Pagan

Road

Shawknowe Ave

Small-burn Dr

Bowl Grn

Kames Motorsport Complex

Harwood Ave

Hawkshaw Terrace

Kames Hill

A70
To Cumnock

Covenanting & Heritage Monument

Kames

Dismantled Railway

Ironworks Cotts

Dismantled

Clubhouse

Garpel Water

Kames Golf Course

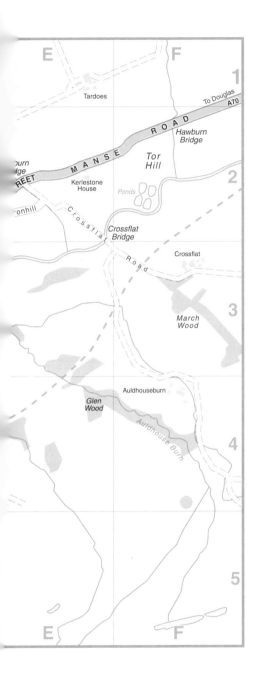

Index to Muirkirk

Bridge Street	E2
Burns Avenue	D3
Cairn View	D3
Carruthers Park	D2
Colthart Drive	B3
Crossflat Road	E2
Furnace Road	D3
Garpel Avenue	B4
Garronhill	E2
Glasgow Road	D3
Hareshaw Crescent	A4
Harwood Avenue	A4
Hawkshaw Terrace	B4
Henderson Drive	B4
Ironworks Cottages	D5
Jacks Mews	E2
Kirk Green	E2
Lapraik Avenue	B3
Lovedale Crescent	D3
Main Street	D3
Manse Road	E2
Meanlour Drive	A4
Middlefield Drive	D2
Miller's Road	B3
Pagan Walk	B4
Park Avenue	D3
Shawknowe Avenue	A4
Smallburn Drive	B4
Smallburn Road	C4
Steven Crescent	D3
Stitt Place	B4
Stoneyhill Avenue	B4
Style, The	D2
Wardlaw Avenue	B4
Wellwood Avenue	D2
Wellwood Street	D2

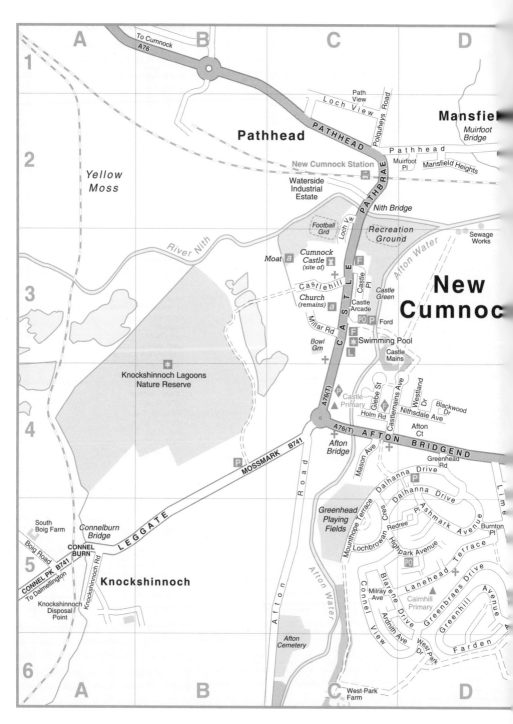

To Cumnock
A76

Pathhead

PATHHEAD

Path View
Loch View
Polquheys Road

Mansfiel
Muirfoot Bridge

Yellow Moss

Pathhead

New Cumnock Station

Muirfoot Pl
Mansfield Heights

Waterside Industrial Estate

PATHBRAE

Nith Bridge

River Nith

Football Grd

Loch Vw

Recreation Ground

Afton Water

Sewage Works

Moat
Cumnock Castle
(site of)

Castlehill
Church
(remains)

F
Castle Pl

Castle Green

New Cumnoc

Castle Arcade
PO P
Ford

Millar Rd

CASTLE

F
L
Swimming Pool

Bowl Grn

Castle Mains

Knockshinnoch Lagoons Nature Reserve

Glebe St
Westland Dr
Blackwood Dr

Castlemains Ave

Nithsdale Ave

A76(T)
P
Castle Primary

Holm Rd

Afton Ct

A76(T)
AFTON BRIDGEND

Greenhead Rd

MOSSMARK B741
P

Afton Bridge

Mason Ave

Dalhanna Drive

Dalhanna Drive

Lime

LEGGATE

Greenhead Playing Fields

Mounthope Terrace

Redree
Cres

Highpark Avenue
Ashmark Avenue

Burnton Pl

South Boig Farm
Connelburn Bridge

Lochbrowan

PO

Boig Road
CONNEL BURN
B741
CONNEL PK

Knockshinnoch Rd

Afton

Afton Water

Milray Ave

Connel Drive

Ardnith Ave

Blarene Terrace

Laneherad Terrace

Greenbraes Drive

Greenhill

Farden

Avenue

To Dalmellington

Knockshinnoch

Knockshinnoch Disposal Point

Cairnhill Primary

Connel View

West Park Dr

Afton Cemetery

West-Park Farm

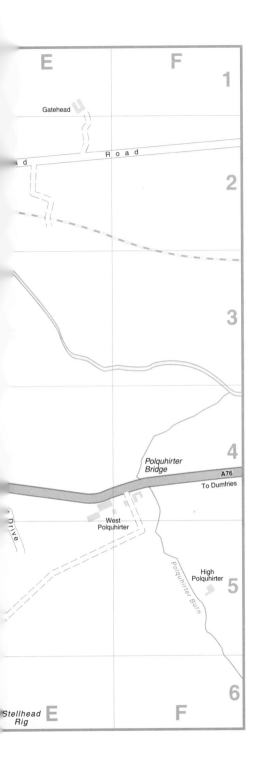

Index to New Cumnock

Afton Bridgend	C4
Afton Court	D4
Afton Road	C5
Ardnith Avenue	C5
Ashmark Avenue	D5
Blackwood Drive	D4
Blarene Drive	C5
Boig Road	A5
Burnton Place	D5
Cairnhill Place	D4
Castle Arcade	C3
Castle Place	C3
Castlehill	C3
Castlemains Avenue	C4
Connel Burn	A5
Connel Park	A5
Connel View	C5
Dalhanna Drive	D4
Farden Avenue	D6
Glebe Street	C4
Glenafton Drive	D5
Greenbraes Drive	D5
Greenhead Road	D4
Greenhill Avenue	D5
Hamilton Drive	E4
High Park Avenue	D5
Holm Road	C4
Knockshinnoch Road	A5
Lanehead Terrace	D5
Leggate	A5
Lime Road	D4
Loch View	C3
Lochbrowan Crescent	C5
Mansfield Court	D2
Mansfield Heights	D2
Mansfield Road	D2
Mason Avenue	C4
Millar Road	C3
Milray Avenue	C5
Mossmark	B4
Mounthope Terrace	C5
Muirfoot Place	D2
Nithsdale Avenue	D4
Pathbrae	C2
Pathhead	C2
Path View	C2
Polquheys Road	C2
Redree Place	D5
Stellhead Avenue	E5
West Park Drive	D6
Westland Drive	D4

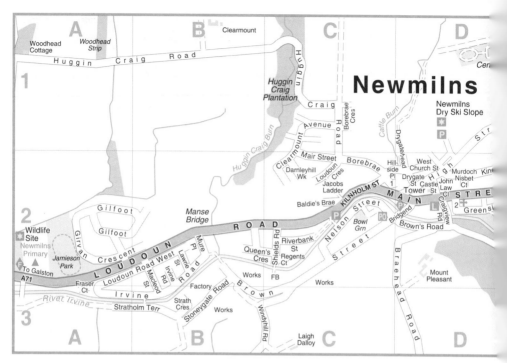

Newmilns

A — Woodhead Cottage, Woodhead Strip, Clearmount
Huggin Craig Road
Huggin Craig Plantation
Huggin Craig Burn

B — Clearmount, Craig Avenue, Borebrae Cres
Mair Street, Borebrae
Clearmount, Damleyhill Wk, Loudoun Cres, Jacobs Ladder
Newmilns Dry Ski Slope
Hillside, West Church St, Drygate St, John Tower St, Castle St, Murdoch, Nisbet Ct, King, Law Cl
Baldie's Brae, Cattle Burn, Dryggatehead
KILNHOLM ST, MAIN STREET, High St, Craigview Rd, Greens

Gilfoot, Gilfoot, Manse Bridge
Girvan Crescent, LOUDOUN ROAD
Wildlife Site, Newmilns Primary, Jamieson Park
To Galston A71
Fraser Ct, Loudoun Road West, Macleod St, Irvine
Mure Pl, Lawrie Rd, Irvine Rd
Shields Rd, Queen's Cres, Regents Ct, Riverbank St
Nelson Street, Bowl Grn, Bridgend, Brown's Road
PO
Braehead Road
Mount Pleasant

River Irvine
Irvine, Strath Cres, Stratholm Terr, Stoneygate Road, Factory, Works
Brown Street, Windyhill Rd, Works, Works
Laigh Dalloy

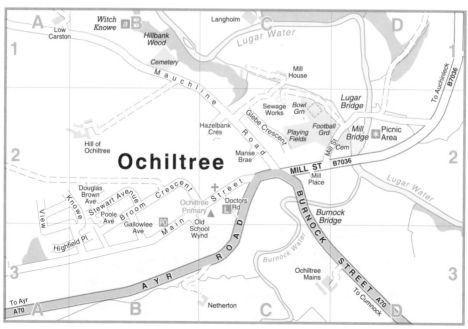

Ochiltree

Low Carston, Witch Knowe, Hillbank Wood
Langholm
Lugar Water
Mauchline
Cemetery
Mill House
Lugar Bridge
To Auchinleck B7036

Hill of Ochiltree
Hazelbank Cres
Glebe Crescent, Sewage Works, Bowl Grn, Playing Fields, Football Grd
Mill St, Cem, Mill Bridge, Picnic Area
Lugar Water
Manse Brae
MILL ST B7036
Mill Place

Douglas Brown Ave, Stewart Avenue, Broom Crescent
Knowe, Poole Ave, Gallowlee Ave
View, Highfield Pl, Main Street
Ochiltree Primary, Doctors Rd
Old School Wynd
AYR ROAD
BURNOCK STREET A70
Burnock Bridge
Burnock Water
Ochiltree Mains
To Cumnock

To Ayr A70
Netherton

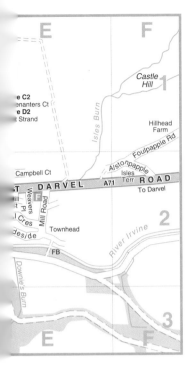

Index to Newmilns

Alstonpapple	F2
Baldies Brae	C2
Borebrae	C2
Borebrae Crescent	C1
Braehead Road	D2
Bridgend	D2
Brown Street	B2
Browns Road	D2
Burn Road	D2
Campbell Court	E2
Campbell Street	E2
Castle Street	D2
Clearmount Avenue	C2
Cochrane Place	E2
Covenanters Court (1)	C2
Craigview Road	D2
Dalwhatswood Road	E1
Darnleyhill Walk	C2
Darvel Road	E2
Drygate Street	D2
Drygatehead	D1
East Church Court	D1
East Strand (2)	D2
Foulpapple Road	F2
Fraser Court	A3
Gilfoot	A2
Girvan Crescent	A2
Greenhead	D2
Greenside	D2
High Street	D2
Hillside Place	C2
Huggin Craig Road	C1
Irvine Road	A3
Isles Street	E2
Isles Terrace	F2
Jacobs Ladder	C2
John Law Close	D2
Kilnholm Street	C2
Kings Crescent	D2
King Street	D2
Ladeside	E2
Lawrie Street	B2
Loudoun Crescent	C2
Loudoun Road	A2
Loudoun Road West	A2
MacLeod Street	B2
Main Street	C2
Mair Street	C2
Mill Court	E2
Mill Crescent	E2
Mill Road	E2
Murdoch Nisbet Court	D2
Mure Place	B2
Nelson Street	C2
Persian Sands	D2
Queens Crescent	B2
Regents Court	C2
Riverbank Street	C2
Shields Road	C2
Stoneygate Road	B3
Strath Crescent	B3
Stratholm Terrace	A3
Townhead	E2
Union Street	E2
Weavers Place	E2
West Campbell Street	E2
West Church Street	D2
Windyhill Road	C3

Index to Ochiltree

Ayr Road	B3
Broom Crescent	B2
Burnock Street	C2
Doctors Road	C2
Douglas Brown Avenue	B2
Gallowlee Avenue	B3
Glebe Crescent	C2
Hazelbank Crescent	C2
Highfield Place	A3
Knowe View	B2
Main Street	B3
Manse Brae	C2
Mauchline Road	B1
Mill Place	C2
Mill Street	C2
Old School Wynd	B3
Poole Avenue	B2
Stewart Avenue	B2

Index to Sorn

Anderson Crescent	B1
Dalgain Drive	C2
Dalyearnoch Road	B1
Fir Park	B1
Main Street	C2
Old Avenue	B2
Treebank Cottages	B1
Woodlands Road	C1
Woolmill Place	C2

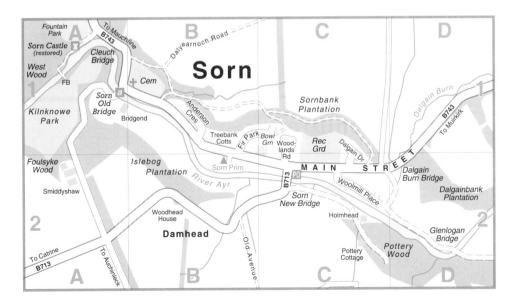

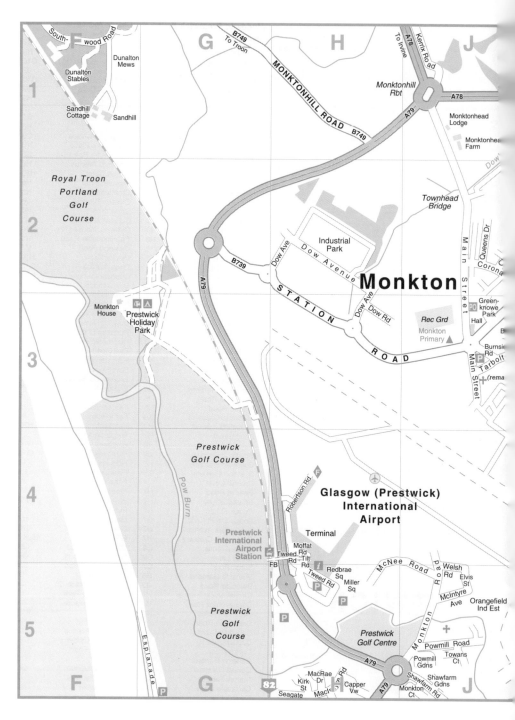

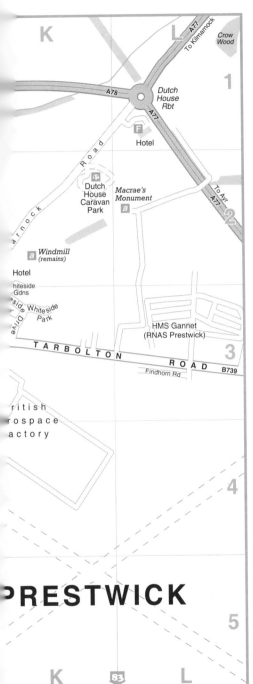

Index to Prestwick & Monkton

Abbot Court	J10
Adamton Road North	J7
Adamton Road South	H9
Adamton Terrace	H8
Afton Avenue	H10
Ailsa Street	G7
Aitkenbrae Drive	J7
Albyn Court	H7
Alexandra Avenue	H6
Alexandra Court	H6
Allanvale Road	G7
Alvord Avenue	J6
Anderson Crescent	K8
Angus Avenue	J7
Annfield Road	G7
Annfield Terrace	G7
Ardayre Road	G7
Ardfin Court	H9
Ardfin Road	H10
Arran Park	G10
Auchincruive Avenue	H8
Ayr Road	G8, G10
Baird Place	J3
Baird Road	J3
Bank Street	G7
Barnweil Avenue	H9
Barony Road	H9
Bellevue Crescent	H8
Bellevue Road	H7
Bellfield Lane	G7
Bellrock Avenue	G10
Benmore	H10
Bennan House (1)	G10
Bennoch Place	J10
Bentfield Drive	G10
Berelands Avenue	J7
Berelands Gardens	J6
Berelands Road	J6
Biggart Road	H8
Blackford Crescent	K6
Blanefield Avenue	H9
Boyd Street	H7
Boydfield Avenue	H6
Boydfield Court	J7
Boydfield Gardens	H6
Brandon Gardens	G8
Briarhill Court	J7
Briarhill Road	H7
Briarhill Street	H7
Bridge Street	G7
Bridge Street Lane	G7
Broompark Avenue	H7
Broompark Crescent	H7
Bruce Avenue	G9
Bruce Lane	G9
Burgh Road	G7
Burnside Gardens	H6
Burnside Road	J3
Caerlaverock Avenue	H7
Caerlaverock Road	H7
Callander Road	J10
Calvinston Road	J10
Cangillan Court	J10
Capper View	H5
Cargill Drive	J10
Carleton Gardens	H8
Carnell Crescent	J8
Carnell Court	J8
Carradale Drive	H10
Carrick Place	G8
Charles Avenue	J2
Clune Drive	J7
Cochrane Place	G7
Coila Avenue	H9
Colonsay House (11)	G10
Coronation Street	J2
Corrie House (2)	G10
Coulthard Drive	J9
Coylebank	H9
Craigfin Court	J10
Craigie Street	G7
Craigneil Drive	H8
Craigpark Avenue	G9
Craigskeen Place	J10
Crandleyhill Road	G9
Crawford Avenue	H9
Creran Court	H10
Crescent, The	H6
Crofthead Road	H6
Crosbie Terrace	J8
Cross, The	H6
Culzean Avenue	J8
Cumbrae House (12)	G10
Cunninghame Road	H8
Dalwood Road	G7
Devilla Court	H10
Doon Avenue	G10
Douglas Avenue	G9
Dow Avenue	H2, H3
Dow Road	H2
Duart Avenue	H7, H8
Duart Crescent	H7
Dunalton Mews	F1
Dunalton Stables	F1
Dundonald Terrace	J8
East Road	J9, H10
Edmiston Avenue	G8
Elvis Street	J5
Englewood Avenue	G10
Esplanade	F7, F8
Fairway View	J9
Farden Place	J9
Farm Road	J6
Fearnoch	H10
Ferguson Avenue	J7
Fernbank	G10
Fernbank Court	G10
Fiddison Place	K10
Findhorn Road	L3
Firhill Drive	J2
Fresson Avenue	L7
Fullarton Road	H9
Fulshaw Court	J10
Gardiner Street	H7
Garryhorn	J10
Glenburn Road	K6, K7
Glenpark Avenue	J9
Grangemuir Court	G8
Grangemuir Road	G8
Gray Street	H7
Greenan Terrace (2)	J8
Greenknowe Park	J3
Greenside Avenue	J8
Gullin Drive	K10
Hamilton Way	H6
Hawthorn Avenue	H8
Hawthorn Gardens	H8
Heathfield Road	G10
Heathpark	H10
Highfield Avenue	J8
Hillside Crescent	J7
Hunter Street	H7

continued overleaf...

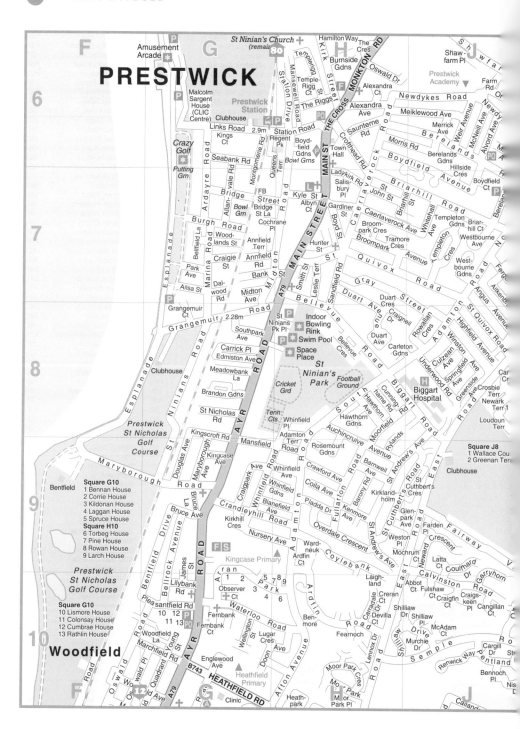

PRESTWICK

Amusement Arcade

St Ninian's Church (remain)

Hamilton Way
The Cres
Shaw-farm Pl

Prestwick Academy

Malcolm Sargent House (CLIC Centre)
Clubhouse

Prestwick Station

Burnside Gdns
Oswald Dr

Alexandra Ct
Alexandra Ave

Newdykes Road
Meiklewood Ave

Merrick Ave
Morris Rd
Berelands Gdns
Hillside Cres
Boydfield Ct

Links Road 2.9m
Station Road

Kings Ct
Seabank Rd
Regent Pk
Boyd-field Gdns
Bowl Grns
Town Hall

Crazy Golf
Putting Grn

Montgomerie Rd
Queens Terr

Briarhill Road

Ardayre Road
Allanvale Rd
FB
Bridge Street
Bridge St La
Kyle St
Salisbury Pl
Ladykirk Rd
John St
Briarhill St
Templeton Gdns
Briarhill Ct
Westbourne Ave

Bellfield La
Bridge Road
Bowl Grn
Cochrane

Burgh Road
Woodlands St
Annfield Terr
Albyn Ct
Gardiner St
Caerlaverock Ave
Whitehall Ave

Park Ave
Craigie St
Annfield Rd
Hunter St
Broom-park Cres
Tramore Cres
West-bourne Gdns

Ailsa St
Dalwood Rd
Bank St
Midton Ave
Smith St
Leslie Terr
Broompark Ave
Quivox Road
Templeton Cres

Grangemuir Ct
Grangemuir Road 2.28m
Road
Bellevue Road
Gray Street
Duart Ave
Duart Cres
Craigneil
Rowallan Cres
Highfield Ave
Angus Avenue

Southpark Ave
St Ninians Pk Pl
Indoor Bowling Rink
Craignell Dr
Duart Ave
Winston Ave
St Quivox Road

Clubhouse
Carrick Pl
Edmiston Ave
Swim Pool
Space Place
Bellevue Cres
Carleton Gdns
Culzean Ave
Springfield Ave

Meadowbank La
St Ninian's Park
Football Ground
Cunning hame Rd
Hawthorn Rd
Biggart Rd
Underwood Rd
Greenside Rd
Crosbie Terr
Newark Terr

Brandon Gdns
Cricket Grd

St Nicholas Rd
Tenn Cts
Whinfield Pl
South Rd
Hawthorn Gdns
Moorfield Ave
Biggart Hospital
Loudoun Terr

Prestwick St Nicholas Golf Course

Kingscroft Rd
Douglas Ave
Maryborough Ave
Kingcase Ave
Mansfield Road
Adamton Terr
Auchincruive Avenue
Rosemount Gdns
Rylands
St Andrew's Road
Clubhouse

Maryborough Road

Square J8
1 Wallace Cou
2 Greenan Ter

Bentfield
Square G10
1 Bennan House
2 Corrie House
3 Kildonan House
4 Laggan House
5 Spruce House
Square H10
6 Torbeg House
7 Pine House
8 Rowan House
9 Larch House

Bruce Ave
Craigpark Ave
Whinfield Ave
Crawford Ave
Coila Ave
Barnwell Ave
St Cuthbert's Cres
Fairway

Kirkhill Cres
Whinfield Gdns
Blanefield Ave
Pladda Ave
Kenmore Ave
Kirkland-holm Cres
Glen-park Ave
Farden Ct
Crescent

Crandiehill Road
Nursery Ave
Overdale Crescent
Weston Pl
Mochrum Ct
Latta Ct
Coulthard Dr
Garryhorn Road

Prestwick St Nicholas Golf Course

Square G10
10 Lismore House
11 Colonsay House
12 Cumbrae House
13 Rathlin House

James St
Lilybank Rd
Ardfin Ct
Ward-neuk
Kingcase Primary
Coylebank
Laighland
Calvinston Road
Abbot Ct
Fulshaw Ct
Craigfin Ct
Craigs-keen Pl
Cangillan Ct.

Woodfield

Bellrock Avenue
Bentfield Drive
Aran Park
1 2
Observer 3 4 5 6 7 8 9
Ardin Road
Carragdale
Creran Ct
Devilla Dr
Shilliaw Dr
Shilliaw Pl
McAdam Dr
Murchie Dr

Pleasantfield Rd
Fernbank Ct
Waterloo Road
Wellington Rd
Lugar Cres
Ben-more
Lennox Dr
Renwick Way
Pentland
Cargill Dr

Woodfield La
Marchfield Rd
Young Rd
Englewood Ave
Ben-more Road
Fearnoch
Semple Dr
Bennoch Pl

Oswald
Road
Quadrant
Marchfield Dr
B743 HEATHFIELD RD
Heathfield Primary
Alton Avenue
Moor Park Cres
Moor Park
Moor Park Pl

Clinic
Heath-park

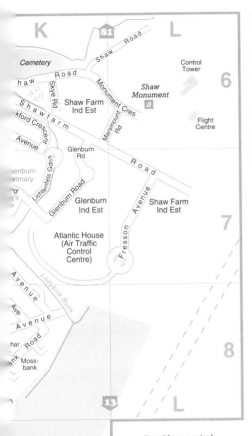

MacIntyre Road	H5	Rylands	H9
MacRae Drive	H5	St Andrew's Avenue	H9
McAdam Court	J10	St Cuthbert's Crescent	J9
McIntyre Avenue	J5	St Cuthbert's Road	H9
McNee Road	H5	St John Street	H7
McNeill Avenue	J6	St Nicholas Road	G8
Main Street (Prestwick)	H7	St Ninians Park Place	H8
Main Street (Monkton)	J3	St Ninians Road	G9
Mansewell Road	H6	St Quivox Road	H7, J8
Mansfield Road	G9	Salisbury Place	H7
Manson Avenue	J6	Sandfield Road	H7
Marchburn Avenue	K7	Sanquhar Avenue	K8
Marchfield Quadrant	G10	Saunterne Road	H6
Marchfield Road	G10	Seabank Road	G6
Marina Road	G7	Seagate	H5
Marsmount Road	L6	Semple Road	J10
Maryborough Avenue	G9	Shaw Road	K6
Maryborough Road	F9	Shawfarm Court	J6
Meadowbank Lane	G8	Shawfarm Gardens	J5
Meiklewood Avenue	H6	Shawfarm Place	J6
Merrick Avenue	J6	Shawfarm Road	J5, K6
Midton Avenue	G7	Sherwood Road	K7
Midton Road	H7	Shilliaw Drive	J10
Miller Square	H5	Shilliaw Place	J10
Mochrum Court	J9	Skye Road	K6
Moffat Road	H4	Smith Street	H7
Monkton Court	J5	Southpark Avenue	G8
Monkton Road	H6, J5	Southwood Road	F1
Monktonhill Road	H1	Springfield Avenue	J8
Montgomerie Road	G7	Spruce House (5)	G10
Monument Crescent	K6	Station Drive	H6
Moor Park	H10	Station Road (Prestwick)	H6
Moor Park Crescent	H10	Station Road (Monkton)	H2
Moor Park Place	H10	Strang Place	J10
Moorfield Road	H8	Tarbolton Road	K3
Morris Road	H6	Tay Road	H4
Mossbank	K8	Templerigg Court	H6
Murchie Drive	J10	Templerigg Street	H6
Neward Crescent	J9	Templeton Crescent	J7
Newark Terrace	J8	Templeton Gardens	J7
Newdykes Court	J6	Tilt Road	H4
Newdykes Road	J6	Torbeg House (6)	H10
Nisbet Drive	J10	Towans Court	J5
Nursery Avenue	G9	Tramore Crescent	H7
Obree Avenue	J10	Tweed Road	H4
Observer Court	G10	Underwood Road	J8
Orangefield Drive	J6	Wallace Court (1)	J8
Oswald Drive	H6	Wardneuk	H9
Oswald Place	F10	Waterloo Road	G10
Oswald Road	F10	Weir Avenue	J6
Outdale Avenue	K7	Wellington Street	G10
Overdale Crescent	H9	Welsh Road	J5
Park Avenue	G7	Westbourne Avenue	J7
Pentland Drive	J10	Westbourne Gardens	J7
Pine House (7)	H10	Weston Place	H9
Pladda Drive	H9	Whinfield Avenue	H9
Pleasantfield Road	G10	Whinfield Gardens	H9
Powmill Gardens	J5	Whinfield Place	H8
Powmill Road	J5	Whinfield Road	G9
Queens Drive	J2	Whitehall Avenue	J7
Queens Terrace	G6	Whiteside Drive	K3
Raith Avenue	K8	Whiteside Gardens	K3
Raith Terrace	K8	Whiteside Park	K3
Rathlin House (13)	G10	Whiteside Place	K3
Redbrae Square	H5	Whiteside Road	J8
Regent Park	H6	Whiteside Terrace	J8
Renwick Way	J10	Winston Avenue	J8
Riggs, The	H6	Wood Park	H8
Robertson Road	H4	Woodfield Avenue	F10
Rosemount Gardens	H9	Woodfield Lane	G10
Rowallan Crescent	J8	Woodlands Street	G7
Rowan House (8)	H9	Young Street	G10
Rowanbank Road	K8	Younger Drive	H5

continued from overleaf...

Indale Avenue	J8
James Street	G10
Kenmore Avenue	H9
Kerrix Road	J1
Kildonan House (3)	G10
Kilmarnock Road	K2
Kingcase Avenue	G9
Kings Court	G6
Kingscroft Road	G8
Kirk Street	H5, H6
Kirkhill Crescent	G9
Kirklandholm	H9
Kyle Street	H7
Ladykirk Road	H7
Laggan House (4)	G10
Laighland	H10
Langcroft Avenue	K6
Larch House (9)	H10
Latta Court	J9
Lennox Drive	H10
Leslie Terrace	H7
Lichtenfels Gardens	K7
Lilybank Road	G10
Links Road	G6
Lismore House (10)	G10
Loudon Terrace	J8
Lugar Crescent	G10

Cemetery

Shaw Road

Shaw Road

Shaw Monument **a**

Control Tower

Flight Centre

Monument Cres

Shaw Farm Ind Est

Skye Rd

Shawfarm

kford Crescent

Avenue

Glenburn Rd

Road

Marsmount Rd

Lichtenfels Gdns

Glenburn Road

Glenburn Ind Est

Fresson Avenue

Shaw Farm Ind Est

Atlantic House (Air Traffic Control Centre)

Ladykirk Burn

Avenue

Avenue

Road

Moss-bank

Avenue

Avenue

K

L

6

7

8

9

10

81

13

stwick
uthbert
Golf
ourse

K

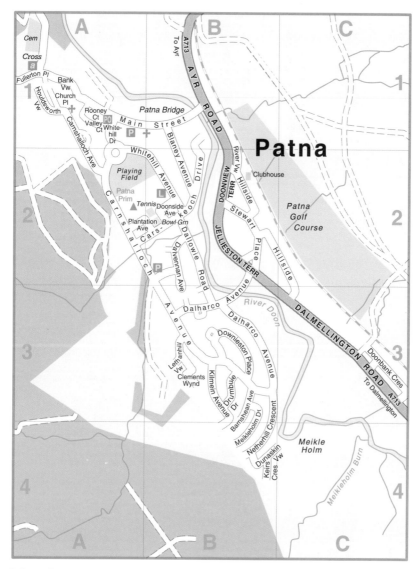

Index to Patna

Ayr Road	B1	Doonbank Crescent	C3	Lethanhill View	B3
Bank View	A1	Doonside Avenue	B2	Main Street	A1
Barnshean Avenue	B3	Doonview Terrace	B2	Meikleholm Drive	B4
Blaney Avenue	B2	Downieston Place	B3	Netherhill Crescent	B4
Carnshalloch Avenue	A1, A2	Drumbuie Drive	B3	Plantation Avenue	A2
Carskeoch Drive	B2	Dunaskin View	B4	River View	B2
Church Place	A1	Fullerton Place	A1	Rooney Court	A1
Clements Wynd	B3	Hillside	B2	Stewart Place	B2
Dalharco Avenue	B3	Houldsworth View	A1	Valley Court	A1
Dallowie Road	B2	Jellieston Terrace	B2	Whitehill Avenue	A2
Dalmellington Road	C3	Keirs Crescent	B4	Whitehill Drive	A1
Dalvennan Avenue	B2	Kilmein Avenue	B3		

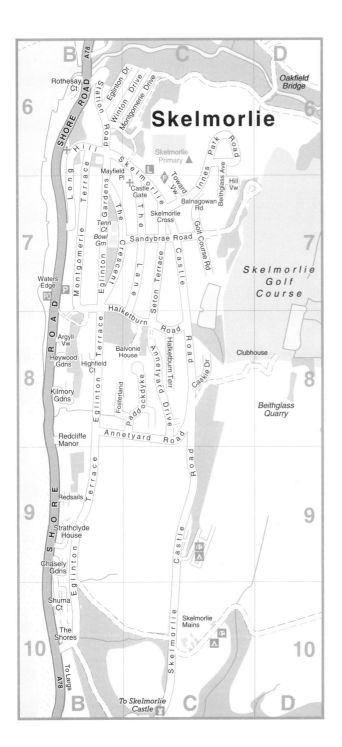

Skelmorlie

Index to Skelmorlie

Annetyard Drive	C8
Annetyard Road	C8
Argyll View	B8
Balnagowan Road	C7
Balvonie House	B8
Beithglass Avenue	C7
Caskie Drive	C8
Castle Gate	C7
Chasely Gardens	B9
Crescent, The	B7
Eglinton Drive	B6
Eglinton Gardens	B7
Eglinton Terrace	B8, B9
Fosterland	C8
Golf Course Road	C7
Halketburn Road	C8
Halketburn Terrace	C8
Heywood Gardens	B8
Highfield Court	B8
Hill View	C7
Innes Park Road	C7
Kilmory Gardens	B8
Lane, The	C7
Long Hill	B7
Mayfield Place	B6
Montgomerie Drive	C6
Montgomerie Terrace	B7
Paddockdyke	C8
Redcliffe Manor	B8
Redsails	B9
Rothesay Court	B6
Sandybrae Road	C7
Seton Terrace	C7
Shore Road	B6, B9
Shores, The	B10
Shuma Court	B10
Skelmorlie Castle Road	C7, C10
Skelmorlie Cross	C7
Station Road	B6
Strathclyde House	B9
Toward View	C7
Waters Edge	B7
Winton Drive	B6

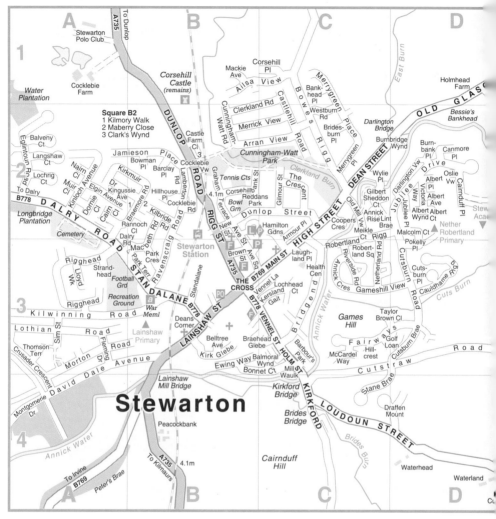

Stewarton

Index to Stewarton

Ailsa View	B1	Bowes Rigg	C1	Corsehill Place	C1	Fairways	C
Albert Avenue	D2	Bowman Place	B2	Crusader Crescent	A3	Fleming Drive	A
Albert Court	D2	Braehead Glebe	C3	Crescent, The	C2	Gameshill View	C
Albert Place	D2	Braemore Road	A3	Cross, The	B3	Gilbert Sheddon Court	C
Albert Wynd	D2	Bridesburn Place	C2	CunninghamWatt Road	B2	Gilmour Street	C
Annick Bank	D1	Bridgend	C3	Cutsburn Brae	D3	Golf Loan	D
Annick Crescent	C3	Brown Street	B3	Cutsburn Place	D3	Graham Terrace	B
Annick Rise	C2	Burnbank Place	D2	Cutsburn Road	D3	Hamilton Gardens	C
Armour Place	C2	Burnbridge Wynd	C2	Cutstraw Road	C3	High Street	C
Arran View	B2	Cairn Close	A2	Dalry Road	A2	Hillcrest	C
Avenue Square	B3	Cairnduff Place	D2	Darlington View	D2	Hillhouse Place	B
Avenue Street	B2	Canmore Place	D2	David Dale Avenue	A4	Holmhead Drive	D1
Balmoral Wynd	C3	Castle Farm Close	B2	Dean Street	C2	Holm Street	C
Balveny Court	A2	Castlehill Road	C2	Deans Corner	B3	Jamieson Place	A
Bankhead Place	C1	Cauldhame Rigg	D3	Dornie Close	A2	Jubilee Drive	D2
Barbour's Park	C3	Clark's Wynd (3)	B2	Draffen Mount	D4	Jubilee Place	D2
Barclay Place	B2	Clerkland Road	B2	Dunlop Road	B2	Kersland Gate	C3
Belltree Avenue	B3	Cocklebie Road	B2	Dunlop Street	B2	Kilbride Road	B
Bonnet Court	B3	Cocklebie Vw	B2	Eglintoun Road	A2	Kilmory Walk (1)	B2
		Coopers Crescent	C2	Elgin Avenue	A2	Kilwinning Road	A3
		Corsehillbank Street	B2	Ewing Way	B3	Kingussie Avenue	A2

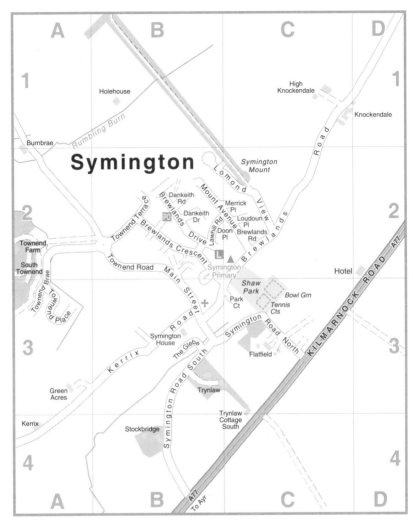

Symington

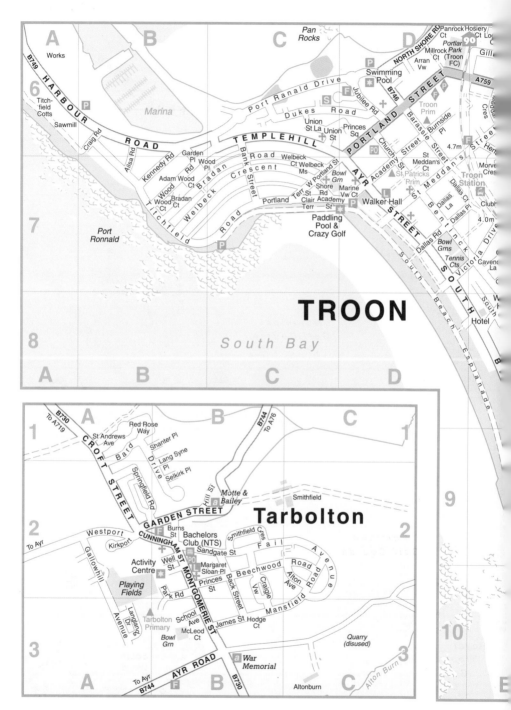

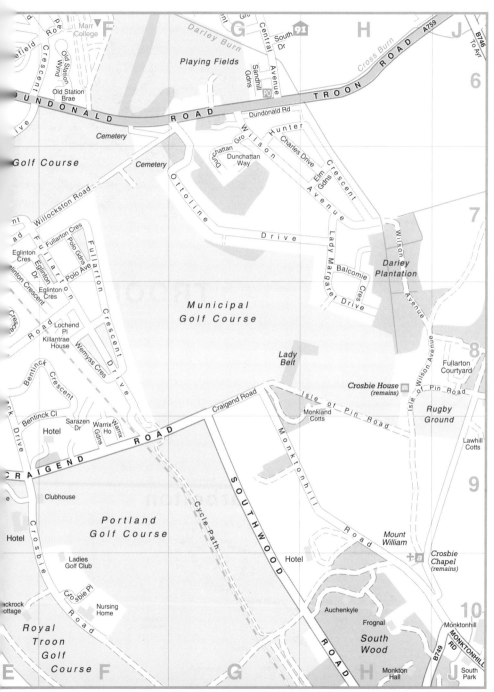

Marr College

Playing Fields

Darley Burn

Central Avenue

South Dr

Cross Burn

To Ayr

A759

B746

Old Station Wynd

Old Station Brae

Sandhill Gdns

PO

DUNDONALD ROAD

TROON ROAD

Cemetery

Golf Course

Cemetery

Dundonald Rd

Willockston Road

Ottoline

Dunchattan Way

Hunter

Charles Drive

Wilson Gro

Elm Gdns

Crescent

Avenue

Drive

Eglinton Cres

Fullarton Cres

Polo Gdns

Polo Ave

Fullarton

Crescent

Drive

Eglinton Cres

Eglinton Crescent

Eglinton Dr

Eglinton Cres

Lochend Pl

Killantrae House

Wemyss Cres

Municipal Golf Course

Lady Margaret Drive

Balcomie Cres

Darley Plantation

Wilson Avenue

Lady Belt

Crosbie House (remains)

Fullarton Courtyard

Isle of Pin Road

Wilson Avenue

Bentinck Crescent

Bentinck Cl

Sarazen Dr

Warrix Gdns

Warrix Ho

Hotel

CRAIGEND ROAD

Craigend Road

Monkland Cotts

Isle of Pin Road

Rugby Ground

Lawhill Cotts

Clubhouse

Portland Golf Course

Cycle Path

SOUTHWOOD ROAD

Monktonhill Road

Hotel

Mount William

Crosbie Chapel (remains)

Hotel

Crosbie Road

Ladies Golf Club

Crosbie Pl

Nursing Home

ackrock ottage

Royal Troon Golf Course

Auchenkyle

Frognal

South Wood

ROAD

Monkton Hall

Monktonhill

MONKTONHILL RD

B749

South Park

E F G H J

Index to street names for Tarbolton & Troon can be found starting on page 91

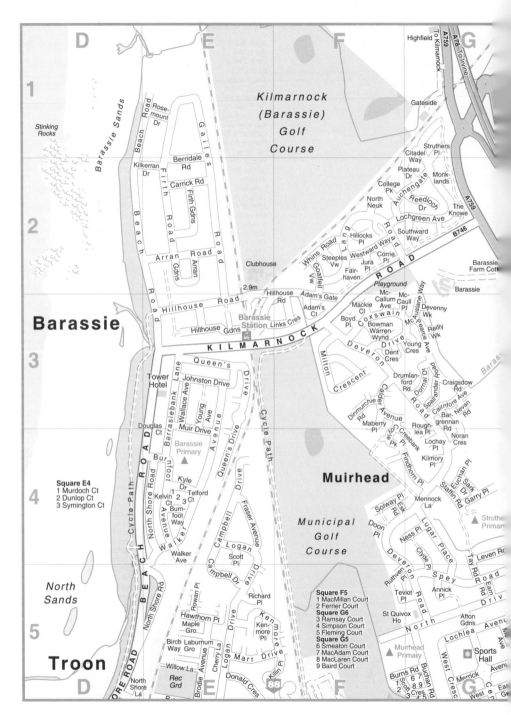

Square E4
1 Murdoch Ct
2 Dunlop Ct
3 Symington Ct

Square F5
1 MacMillan Court
2 Ferrier Court
Square G6
3 Ramsay Court
4 Simpson Court
5 Fleming Court
Square G5
6 Smeaton Court
7 MacAdam Court
8 MacLaren Court
9 Baird Court

Index to Tarbolton

Alton Avenue	C2
Ayr Road	B3
Back Street	B2
Bard Drive	A1
Beechwood Road	B3
Burns Street	B3
Craigie View	B3
Croft Street	A1
Cunningham Street	B3
Fail Avenue	B3
Gallowhill Avenue	A3
Garden Street	B3
Hill Street	B2
Hodge Court	B3
James Street	B3
Kirkport	A3
Langlands Drive	A3
Lang Syne Place	B2
Mcleod Court	B3
Mansefield Road	B3
Margaret Sloan Place	B3
Montgomerie Street	B3
Park Road	B2
Princes Street	B2
Red Rose Way	A1
St Andrews Avenue	A1
Sandgate Street	B3
School Avenue	B3
Selkirk Place	B2
Shanter Place	B1
Smithfield Crescent	B2
Springfield Road	A2
Well Street	B2
Westport	A2

Index to Troon

Academy Street	D7
Adams Court	F3
Adam's Gate	F3
Adam Wood Court	B7
Afton Gardens	G5
Ailsa Road	B7
Aldersyde Avenue	G5
Annick Place	G5
Arran Gardens	E2
Arran Road	E2
Arran View	D6
Auchengate	F2
Ayr Street	D7
Baird Court (9)	G5
Balcomie Crescent	H7
Bank Street	C7
Barassie Farm Cottages	G2
Barassie Street	D6
Barassiebank Lane	E3
Bargrennan Road	G3
Beach Road	D1, D5
Beechwood Paddock	J5
Bentinck Close	E9
Bentinck Crescent	F8
Bentinck Drive	D7, E8
Berriedale Road	E2
Birch Way	E5
Bowman Warren Wynd	F3
Boyd Place	F3
Bradan Court	B7
Bradan Road	C7
Brodie Avenue	E5
Brown Avenue	E6
Buchan Court	G5
Burnfoot Avenue	E4
Burnfoot Way	E4
Burns Road	F5
Burnside Place	D6
Cairnfore Avenue	G3
Calder Avenue	F3
Campbell Drive	E4
Carrick Road	E2
Cavendish Court	E7
Cavendish Lane	E7
Cavendish Place	E7
Central Avenue	G6
Cessnock Road	E6
Chapelhill Cottages	H2
Charles Drive	G6
Cherry Lane	E5
Church Street	D6
Citadel Way	G1
Clyde Place	G4
College Park	F2
Collenan Avenue	H5
Collins Drive	H5
Corrie Place	F2
Coxswain Drive	F3
Coyle Park	F4
Craig Road	B6
Craigend Road	E9, G8
Craigsdow Road	G3
Craiksland Place	H5
Craiksland Road	J5
Creebank Place	F4
Crosbie Court	E9
Crosbie Place	F10
Crosbie Road	E9
Crossburn Drive	J5
Crossburn Lane	J5
Crossburn Terrace	J5
Crummieholm Gardens	H5
Dallas Court	D7
Dallas Lane	D7
Dallas Place	D7
Dallas Road	D7
Darley Crescent	E8
Darley Place	E8
Dent Crescent	F3
Devenny Walk	G3
Deveron Road	F3, F4
Dinmurchie Road	F3
Donald Crescent	E5
Doon Place	F4
Dornal Drive	G3
Douglas Court	E3
Drumlanford Road	G3
Dukes Road	C6
Dunchattan Grove	G7
Dunchattan Way	G7
Dundonald Road	F6
Dunlop Court (2)	E4
Earn Road	G5
East Grove	G5
Eglinton Crescent	E7
Eglinton Drive	F7
Elm Gardens	H7
Esk Road	F4
Euchan Place	G4
Fairhaven	F2
Ferrier Court (2)	F5
Findhorn Place	G4
Firth Gardens	E2
Firth Road	E2
Fleming Court (5)	G5
Fraser Avenue	E4
Fullarton Courtyard	J8
Fullarton Crescent	F7
Fullarton Drive	F8
Fullarton Place	J5

continued overleaf...

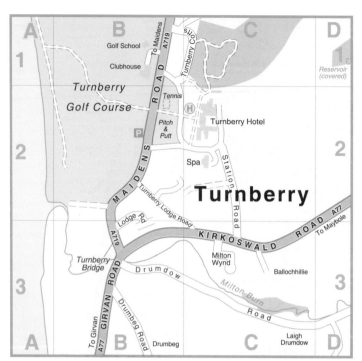

		Sandilands	E			
		Sarazen Drive	F			
		Sark Drive	G			
		Scott Crescent	G			
		Scott Place	E			
		Seaview Terrace	H			
		Shore Road	C			
		Simpson Court (4)	G			
		Smeaton Court (6)	G			
		Solway Place	F			
		South Beach	D7			
		Esplanade				
		South Beach Lane	E8			
		South Beach	D7			
		South Drive	G6			
		Southward Way	G2			
		Southwood Road	G9			
		Spallander Road	G3			
		Spey Road	G5			
		Stable Wynd	J5			
		Staffin Road	G4			
		Steeples View	F2			
		Struthers Place	G1			
		Symington Court (3)	E4			
		Tay Road	G4			
		Telford Court	E4			
		Templehill	C6			
		Teviot Place	F5			
		Titchfield Cottages	A6			
		Titchfield Road	B7			
		Troon Road	H6			
		Union Street	C6			
		Union Street Lane	C6			
		Victoria Drive	E7			
		Walker Avenue	E4			
		Wallace Avenue	E3			
		Wallacefield Road	E6			
		Wardlaw Crescent	H4			
		Warrix Gardens	F9			
		Warrix House	F9			

continued from overleaf...

		Lady Margaret Drive	H7	Murdoch Court (1)	E4
		Lang Road	F2	Ness Place	G4
Gailes Road	E1	Lawhill Cottages	J9	Nevan Road	G3
Garden Place	B6	Leven Road	G4	Noran Crescent	G4
Garry Place	G4	Links Crescent	F3	North Drive	G5
Gillies Street	E6	Lochay Place	G4	North Neuk	F2
Goatfell View	F2	Lochend Place	F8	North Shore Lane	D5
Golf Crescent	E7	Lochend Road	E8	North Shore Road	D6, E4
Golf Place	E7	Lochgreen Avenue	G2	Old Loans Road	H5, J5
Hall Lane	J5	Lochlea Avenue	G5	Old Station Brae	F6
Harbour Road	A6	Logan Court	E6	Old Station Wynd	F6
Harling Drive	E7	Logan Drive	E4, E6	Ottoline Drive	G7
Hawthorn Place	E5	Lugar Place	G4	Panrock Court	D6
Henderson Road	E6	MacAdam Court (7)	G5	Pearce Avenue	G3
Hillhouse Gardens	E3	MacLaren Court (8)	G5	Plateau Drive	G2
Hillhouse Road	E3	MacMillan Court (1)	F5	Polo Avenue	F7
Hillocks Place	F2	McAuslane Way	G3	Polo Gardens	F7
Hosiery Court	E6	McCallum Avenue	F3	Port Ranald Drive	C6
Hunter Crescent	G6	McCaull Place	F3	Portland Street	D6
Isle of Pin Road	H8	Maberry Place	F3	Portland Terrace	C7
Johnston Drive	E3	Mackie Close	F3	Princes Square	D6
Jubilee Road	D6	Main Street	J5	Queens Drive	E3, E4
Jura Place	F2	Maple Grove	E5	Ramsay Court (3)	G5
Kelvin Court	E4	Marine View Court	D7	Reedloch Drive	G2
Kenmore Place	E5	Marr Drive	E5	Reilly Walk	G3
Kenmore	E5	Mennock Lane	G4	Richard Place	E5
Kennedy Road	B7	Merrick Avenue	G5	Rosemount Drive	E1
Kilkerran Drive	E2	Millrock Court	D6	Roughlea Place	G4
Killantrae House	F8	Milton Crescent	F3	Rowan Place	E5
Killin Place	F5	Monkland Cottages	H8	Ruthven Place	F5
Kilmarnock Road	E3	Monklands	G2	St Clair Terrace	C7
Kilmory Place	G4	Monktonhill Road	G9, J10	St Quivox House	G5
Knowe, The	G2	Morven Crescent	E7	St Meddan's Court	D7
Kyle Crescent	H5	Morven Drive	E6	St Meddan's Crescent	E6
Kyle Drive	E4	Mossgiel Avenue	G5	St Meddan's Street	D7
Laburnum Grove	E5	Muir Drive	E4	Sandhill Gardens	G6

Welbeck Court	C7		
Welbeck Crescent	C7		
Welbeck Mews	C7		
Wemyss Crescent	F8		
West Crescent	G5		
West Grove	G5		
West Portland Street	C7		
Westward Way	F2		
Whins Road	F2		
Willockston Road	F7		
Willow Lane	E5		
Wilson Avenue	G6, H8		
Wood Court	B7		
Wood Place	B7		
Wood Road	B7		
Yorke Road	E7		
Young Avenue	E3		
Young Crescent	G3		

Index to Turnberry

Drumbeg Road	B3
Drumdow Road	B3
Girvan Road	B3
Kirkoswald Road	C3
Lodge Road	B2
Maidens Road	B2
Milton Wynd	C3
Station Road	C2
Turnberry Cottages	C1
Turnberry Lodge Road	B2

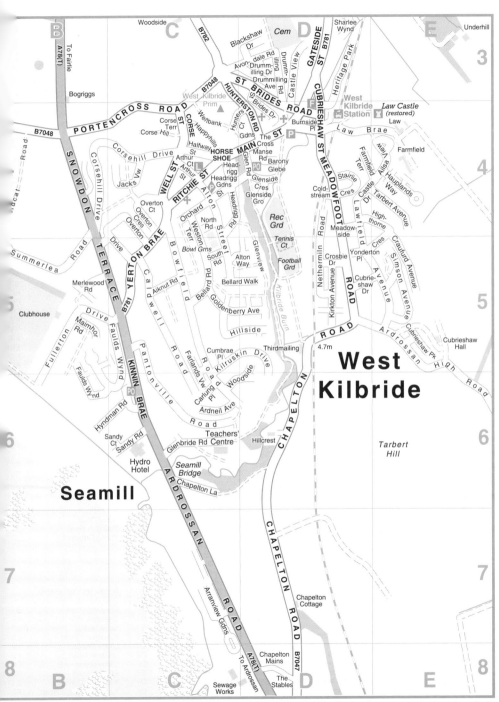

Index to street names can be found overleaf

Index to West Kilbride & Seamill

Aiknut Road	93 C5
Ailsa View	93 E4
Alton Street	93 C4
Alton Way	93 D5
Ardneil Avenue	93 C6
Ardrossan High Road	93 E5
Ardrossan Road	93 C6
Arranview Gardens	93 C7
Arthur Court	93 C4
Arthur Street	93 C4
Avondale Road	93 D3
Barony Glebe	93 D4
Bellard Road	93 C5
Bellard Walk	93 D5
Blackshaw Drive	93 D3
Bowfield Road	93 C5
Burnside Place	93 D4
Caldwell Road	93 C5
Carlung Place	93 C6
Castle Drive	93 D4
Castle View	93 D3
Chapelton Lane	93 C6
Chapelton Mains	93 D8
Chapelton Road	93 D6, D7
Coldstream	93 D4
Corse Hill	93 C4
Corse Street	93 C4
Corse Terrace	93 C4
Corsehill Drive	93 B4, C4
Craufurd Avenue	93 E5
Crosbie Drive	93 D5
Cross, The	93 D4
Cubrieshaw Drive	93 D5
Cubrieshaw Park	93 E5
Cubrieshaw Street	93 D4
Cumbrae Place	93 C5
Drummilling Avenue	93 D3
Drummilling Drive	93 D3
Drummilling Road	93 D3
Farlands View	93 C5
Farmfield Terrace	93 D4
Faulds Wynd	93 C5
Fullerton Drive	93 B5
Gateside Street	93 D3
Glen Road	93 D4
Glenbride Road	93 C6
Glenside Crescent	93 D4
Glenside Grove	93 D4
Glenview	93 D5
Goldenberry Avenue	93 C5
Halfway Street	93 C4
Happyhills	93 C4
Hauplands Way	93 E4
Headrigg Gardens	93 C4
Headrigg Road	93 C4
Headrigg	93 C4
Heritage Park	93 D3
Highthorne Crescent	93 E4
Hillside	93 C5
Horse Shoe	93 C4
Hunters Court	93 C4
Hunterston Road	93 C3
Hyndman Road	93 B6
Jacks View	93 C4
Kilruskin Drive	93 C5
Kinnin Brae	93 C4
Kirkton Avenue	93 D5
Law Brae	93 D4
Lawfield Avenue	93 D5
Maimhor Road	93 B5
Main Street	93 D4
Manse Road	93 D4

Meadowfoot Road	93 D4
Meadowside	93 D4
Merlewood Road	93 B5
Nethermiln Road	93 D5
North Road	93 C4
Orchard Street	93 C4
Overton Court	93 C4
Overton Crescent	93 C4
Overton Drive	93 C4
Pantonville Road	93 C6
Portencross Road	93 B4
Ritchie Street	93 C4
Sandy Court	93 C6
Sandy Road	93 C6
Sharlee Wynd	93 D3
Simson Avenue	93 E5
Snowdon Terrace	93 B4
South Road	93 C5
St Brides Drive	93 D4
St Brides Road	93 D3
Stables, The	93 D8
Stairlie Crescent	93 D4
Summerlea Road	93 B5
Tarbert Avenue	93 E4
Well Street	93 C4
Wellbank Gardens	93 C4
Weston Terrace	93 C4
Wildcat Road	93 B4
Woodside	93 C6
Yerton Brae	93 C5
Yonderton Place	93 D5

Index to Ayr

Abbot Court	13 J10
Abbots Crescent	17 A21
Abbots Way	16 B20
Abercromby Drive	16 C20
Academy Street	14 E14
Afton Avenue	13 H10
Afton Court	15 G17
Ailsa Place	14 D14
Ailsa View	17 A21
Ailsa View Gardens	17 A21
Ailsa View Place	16 B20
Ailsa View Wynd	17 A21
Airlie Court	14 D17
Albert Terrace	14 F15
Alder Bank	15 J17
Alderston Avenue	12 F12
Alderston Park	12 F12
Alderston Place	12 F12
Alexandra Terrace	12 F12
Allan Place	13 H12
Allenfield Road	15 J17
Allison Street	12 F13
Alloway	16 D22
Alloway Park	14 D15
Alloway Place	14 D15
Alloway Place Lane	14 D15
Alloway Street	14 E16
Altry Place	17 A22
Anderson Crescent	17 G19
Annfield Glen Road	17 G19
Annpit Road	12 G11
Ardfin Court	13 H9
Ardfin Road	13 H10
Ardlui Road	12 F11
Argyle Park	12 F13
Armour Drive	15 H17
Arnprior Place	17 E21
Arran Mall	14 E15
Arran Park	12 G10
Arran Terrace	14 D14

Arranview Court	12 G11
Arrol Drive	14 C18, 16 C19
Arrol Park	14 D18
Arthur Street	14 E15
Ashgrove Street	14 F16
Aspen Court	15 J18
Aspen Road	15 J18
Auchenbeg Crescent	17 F20
Auchendoon Crescent	16 C19
Auchentrae Crescent	16 C19
Auld Nick's View	16 D22
Back Hawkhill Avenue	12 G13
Backpeebles Street	12 E13
Baird Road	16 D22
Ballantine Drive	14 E17
Ballantine Drive Lane	14 E17
Balminnoch Park	16 C22
Bankfield Park	17 H20
Barnford Crescent	17 F21
Barns Crescent	14 E15
Barns Park	14 E15
Barns Street	14 E15
Barns Street Lane	14 E15
Barns Terrace	14 E16
Barns Terrace Lane	14 E16
Bath Place	14 D15
Bathurst Drive	17 F22
Beagle Crescent	16 B20
Beech Grove	15 H15
Belleisle Cottages	16 C20
Belleisle Drive	16 C19
Belleisle Wynd	16 C19
Bellesleyhill Avenue	12 G12
Bellesleyhill Court	12 F11
Bellesleyhill Road	12 F11
Bellevale Avenue	14 E18
Bellevale Quadrant	14 E18
Bellevue Cottages	14 E16
Bellevue Crescent	14 E16
Bellevue Lane	14 E16
Bellevue Road	14 E16
Bellevue Street	14 E16
Bellrock Road	12 F11
Belmont Avenue	14 F17, F18
Belmont Crescent	14 F18
Belmont Drive	14 F18
Belmont Place East	14 F17
Belmont Place West	14 F17
Belmont Road	14 F18
Belvidere Terrace	12 F13
Benmore	13 H10
Bennoch Place	13 J10
Bentfield Avenue	14 D17
Beresford Court	14 E16
Beresford Lane	14 E16
Beresford Terrace	14 E16
Birch Road	17 H19
Blackburn Drive	14 C17
Blackburn Place	14 D17
Blackburn Road	14 D17
Blackfriars Court	14 E15
Blackfriars Walk	14 E15
Blackhill Street	15 G18
Blackhouse Place	15 H15
Boat Vennal	14 E14
Boswell Park	14 E15
Boundary Road	13 J11
Bourtree Park	14 F17
Bowman Road	14 E17
Bracken Park	17 H20
Bradan Drive	17 G21
Braehead Avenue	13 H13
Braehead Crescent	15 H14

Braehead Road	13?
Braemar Square	13?
Braeside Road	13?
Briar Grove	17?
Britannia Place	12?
Broadwood Park	17 F21, ?
Broomfield Garden	14?
Broomfield Road	14?
Broun Drive	16?
Browncarrick Drive	17?
Bruce Crescent	14?
Buchan Court (4)	14?
Burnbank Place	17?
Burnbank Road	17?
Burness Avenue	16?
Burnett Terrace	15 C?
Burns Statue Square	14?
Burns' Wicket	16?
Butter Market Close	14?
Cairn Crescent	16 C?
Cairnsmore Drive	16?
Caledonia Road	15 G17, H?
Callander Road	13?
Callendar Place	12 G?
Calvinston Road	13?
Cambusdoon Drive	16 D?
Cambuslea Gardens	12 G?
Cambuslea Road	12 G?
Campbell Court	15 H?
Campbell Street	12 F?
Camphill Place	15 G?
Campion Court	17 G?
Cangillan Court	13 J?
Carcluie Crescent	17 G?
Cargill Drive	13 J?
Carradale Drive	13 H?
Carrick Avenue	14 E?
Carrick Gardens	14 E?
Carrick Park	14 E?
Carrick Road	14 E?
Carrick Road Lane	14 E?
Carrick Street	14 E?
Carseloch Road	17 E2?
Carwinshoch View	14 C1?
Cassillis Street	14 D1?
Castle Square	17 A2?
Castle View	17 A2?
Castle Walk	16 B2?
Castlehill Court	15 G1?
Castlehill Crescent	14 F1?
Castlehill Gardens	15 H1?
Castlehill Road	14 F1?
Cathcart Street	14 E1?
Cedar Road	17 H19, 15 J1?
Celandine Bank	17 H2?
Cessnock Place	15 H1?
Chalmers Avenue	14 E1?
Chalmers Road	14 E17, F17?
Chapelpark Road	14 E18?
Charlotte Street	14 D15?
Charlotte Street Lane	14 D15?
Cherry Hill Road	17 G21
Chestnut Road	15 J17
Church Court	14 F14
Churchill Crescent	15 H15
Churchill Tower	12 D13
Citadel Place	14 D14
Clarendon Place	15 H18
Clarke Avenue	14 D17
Clochranhill Road	16 E21
Cloverhill	15 J17
Content Avenue	14 F15
Content Street	14 F14
Coranbae Place	17 A22

Name	Ref		Name	Ref
...nhill	17 G20		East Road	13 H10
...sehill Park	14 E18		Edenhall Road	12 G11
...sehill Place	14 E18		Eglinton Place	14 D14
...sehill Road	14 E18		Eglinton Terrace	14 D14
...serine Road	17 A22		Elba Court	14 F14
...ton Howe	17 F23		Elba Gardens	14 F14
...rton Lea	17 F23		Elba Street	14 F14
...rton Shaw	17 G23		Ellisland Place	15 G17
...wan Crescent	13 H12		Ellisland Square	15 G17
...aig Drive	17 A21		Elmbank Street	12 E12
...aigfin Court	13 J10		Elms Way	12 G11
...aighall Place	17 F21		Englewood Avenue	12 G10
...aigholm Road	15 J16		Esplanade	16 C19, 14 D15
...aigie Avenue	14 F15		Ettrick Place	12 G11
...aigie Lea	15 G15		Ewenfield Avenue	17 F19
...aigie Road	14 F15		Ewenfield Gardens	17 E19
...aigie Way	15 G15		Ewenfield Park	17 E19
...aigshiel Place	16 C19		Ewenfield Place	17 F19
...aigskeen Place	13 J10		Ewenfield Road	17 E19
...aigstewart Crescent	16 B22		Fairfield Park	14 D16
...aigston Avenue	15 H17		Fairfield Road	14 D16
...aigweil Place	14 D16		Falkland Park Road	12 F12
...aigweil Road	14 D16		Falkland Place	12 F12
...ranesbill Court	17 G20		Falkland Road	12 F12
...reran Court	13 H10		Farrell Place	12 G13
...rocus Bank	17 H20		Fearnoch	13 H10
...rofthead Road	15 H18, J18		Fellhill Street	15 G18
...romwell Road	14 D14		Fenwickland Avenue	17 F19
...ross Street	14 E14		Fenwickland Place	17 G19
...rossburn	17 A22		Ferguson Street	13 H13
...rown Square	12 E13		Fern Brae	17 H20
...rown Street	12 E13		Fernbank	12 G10
...ulzean Road	16 C20		Fernbank Court	12 G10
...unning Park Drive	16 C20		Fiddison Place	13 K10
...unningham Crescent	15 G17		Finlas Avenue	17 G20
...unningham Place	15 H17		Finnick Glen	17 F20
...urtican Place	14 E17		Fir Bank	15 H18
Daisy Cottages	12 F12		Flaxton Court	14 E17
Dalblair Arcade	14 E15		Forbes Drive	13 H11
Dalblair Court	14 E15		Forehill Road	15 H17
Dalblair Road	14 E15		Forest Way	15 H18
Dalblair Way	14 E16		Forge Road	12 G11
Dalmellington Road	15 G18, 17 H19		Fort Court	14 E14
Dalmilling Crescent	13 J13		Fort Street	14 E15
Dalmilling Drive	13 J13		Fotheringham Road	14 F15
Dalmilling Road	13 J13		Foxglove Place	17 H20
Dalton Park	17 A21		Fullarton Street	14 E15
Damside	12 E13		Fulshaw Court	13 J10
Davidson Place	14 F14		Fulshaw Crescent	13 L13
Devilla Court	13 H10		Fulshaw Place	13 K12
Dongola Road	14 F16		Galloway Avenue	13 H13
Doon Avenue	12 G10		Galloway Gardens	13 H13
Doonbank Park	16 C23		Garden Court	14 E14
Doonfoot Road	16 C20, D19		Garden Street	14 E14
Doonholm Road	17 E22		Gartferry Court	14 D17
Doonholm Park	17 E23		Gavin Hamilton Court	15 H17
Doonholm Place	16 E22		Gearholm Road	16 C20
Doonvale Drive	17 F23		Gemmell Court	15 H14
Doonvale Place	17 F23		Gemmell Crescent	15 H14
Doonview Gardens	16 B21		George Place	17 A21
Doonview Wynd	16 B21		George Square	14 F14
Donnini Court (1)	14 D14		George Street	14 F14
Dornoch Park	14 D17		George's Avenue	12 G12
Douglas Lane	14 E15		Glebe Road	12 E13
Douglas Street	14 E15		Glebe Crescent	12 E13
Drumellan Road	17 F21		Glenalla Crescent	16 B22
Drummond Crescent	13 K13		Glencairn Road	15 G17, H17
Duke Street	12 F13		Glenconner Place	15 G17
Dumfries Park	17 F22		Glenconner Road	15 G17
Dunlop Crescent	15 K14		Glendale Crescent	17 G19
Dunlop Place	15 J14		Glendale Place	17 G19
Dunure Road	17 A21, 16 B21		Glenford Place	14 D14
Earls Way	16 B20, B21		Glengall Lane	17 G21
East Park Road	12 G12		Glenmount Place	17 A22

Name	Ref		Name	Ref
Glenmuir Court	13 H13		Kilbrandon Way	17 A21
Glenmuir Place	13 J13		Killoch Place	14 E16
Glenmuir Road	13 J13		Kilnbank Crescent	15 J16
Glenmuir Square	13 J13		Kincaidston Drive	17 G20
Glenpark Place	17 G20		King Street	14 F14
Glenriddel Road	15 G17		Kings Court	14 F14
Gordon Street	12 F12		Kings Park	13 H11
Gordon Terrace	14 F15		Kings Park Drive	13 H11
Gorse Park	17 H20		Kirk Port	14 E15
Goschen Terrace	12 G13		Kirkholm Avenue	12 F11
Goukscroft Court	16 C20		Knoll Park	17 E20
Goukscroft Park	16 C20		Knowe, The	14 E18
Gould Street	12 G13		Knoweholm	16 B21
Gowan Bank Road	17 G21		Kyle Court	14 F16
Gower Place	17 G20		Kyle Street	14 E15
Grange Avenue	17 G21		Laburnum Road	15 H17
Green Street	14 E14		Laigh Mount	17 E22
Green Street Lane	12 E13		Lamford Drive	16 B22
Greenan Grove	17 A21		Landsdowne Road	12 F12
Greenan Park	17 A20		Larchwood Road	17 H19
Greenan Place	16 B20		Larghill Lane	15 G18
Greenan Road	17 A20		Laughlanglen Road	17 F21
Greenan Way	17 A20		Laurel Bank	17 H19
Greenfield Avenue	16 C20		Lawson Street	12 G13
Greentree Park	17 H19		Leeward Park	17 F22
Guiltreehill	17 F22		Lennox Drive	13 H10
Gullin Drive	13 K10		Leslie Crescent	14 F17
Halls Vennal	12 E13		Liberator Drive	13 K11
Hamilton Crescent	14 F17		Lilybank Road	12 G10
Harebell Place	17 G20		Limekiln Road	12 E12
Hartfield Road	14 E18		Limonds Court	14 F14
Harthall	13 K13		Limonds Wynd	14 F14
Hawkhill Avenue	12 G13		Lindsay Street	13 H13
Hawkhill Avenue Lane	14 F14		Lindston Place	17 F21
Hawthorn Drive	17 H19		Linfern Place	17 G20
Hay Hill	15 J15		Lisburn Road	12 F11
Hazelwood Road	14 E17		Loaning, The	17 F21
Heather Park	17 H20		Loch Park	16 B20
Heathfield Road	12 G10		Lochlea Drive	15 G17
Heathfield Road	13 K12		Lochside Road	12 G13, 13 H11
Heathpark	13 H10		Lochside Court	12 G13
High Maybole Road	16 D23		Longbank Drive	17 F19
High Road	13 K12		Longbank Road	17 F19
High Street	14 E14, E15		Longhill Avenue	16 B22, C23
High Thornyflat Wynd	13 K12		Longhill Place	16 C23
Highfield Drive	13 K12		Longlands Park	17 F19
Highfield Road	17 G19		Lorien Court	13 H11
Hilary Crescent	14 F17		Lorne Arcade	14 E15
Hillcroft Crescent	15 G18		Lothian Road	14 F16
Hillfoot Road	15 G18, J17		Low Road	13 K12
Hilltop Place	15 J18		Luath Walk	14 E15
Hollow Park	17 G21		Lugar Crescent	12 G10
Hollow Park Court	17 G21		Lymburn Place	15 G15
Holly Bank	15 J18		MacAdam Place	14 F14
Holmston Crescent	15 H16		MacAdam Square	14 F14
Holmston Drive	15 H17		McAdam Court	13 J10
Holmston Gardens	14 F16		McCall's Avenue	12 F12
Holmston Road	15 G16		McColgan Place	13 H12
Home Farm Road	17 F21		McLean Street	13 H13
Honeysuckle Park	17 G21		McNairston Road	15 K18
Hope Street	14 E14		Main Road	13 J13
Hunter's Avenue	12 G11, G12		Main Street	14 E14
Inkerman Court (6)	14 D14		Mainholm Court	15 K14
Inverkar Road	14 F17		Mainholm Crescent	15 J14
Iris Court	17 H20		Mainholm Road	13 J13, 15 K15
Ivy Place	15 J18		Maple Drive	15 J18
James Brown Avenue	13 J13		Marchfield Quadrant	12 F10
James Campbell Road	15 H15		Marchfield Road	12 G10
James Street (Ayr)	14 F14		Marchmont Road	14 E17
James Street (P'twick)	12 G10		Marchmont Road Lane	14 E16
John Street	14 F14		Marguerite Place	17 H20
Juniper Green	15 J17		Marigold Square	17 G20
Kerse Park	17 G22			
Kilbrandon Crescent	17 A21			

Street	Grid	Street	Grid
Marlborough Court (5)	14 D14	Oswald Road	12 F10, F12
Marlepark	17 F20	Overmills Crescent	15 J16
Maryfield Place	12 G11	Overmills Road	15 J16
Maryfield Road	12 G11	Park Circus Lane	14 E16
Masonhill Place	15 H18	Park Circus	14 E16
Masonhill Road	15 H17	Park Terrace	14 D15
Maybole Road	17 F20	Park View	16 E22
Meadow Park	14 F18	Parkhouse Street	14 E16
Meadow Park Drive	14 F18	Pattle Place	16 E22
Merkland Road	17 F21	Paterson Street	12 G11
Mews Lane	14 D15	Pavilion Road	14 D15
Midton Road	14 E17	Peebles Street	12 E13
Mill Brae	14 F16	Peggieshill Place	15 G18
Mill Brae Court	14 F16	Peggieshill Road	17 G19
Mill Street	14 F15	Pemberton Valley	17 F21
Mill Wynd	14 E15	Pentland Drive	13 J10
Miller Road	14 F16	Philip Square	14 F14
Milton Park	17 G20	Pine Brae	15 H18
Monkwood Place	17 F21	Piperhill	17 F21
Montgomerie Terrace	14 D14	Pleasantfield Road	12 G10
Monument Road	16 E20	Poplar Way	15 J18
Moor Park	13 H10	Portmark Avenue	16 B22
Moor Park Crescent	13 H10	Prestwick Road	12 F12
Moor Park Place	13 H10	Primrose Park	17 H20
Moor Place	13 H11	Princes Court	12 F13
Moor Road	13 H11	Promenade	12 F11
Morrison Gardens	15 G15	Quail Road	12 F11
Morton Avenue	14 F18	Queen Street	14 F14
Morton Road	14 F18	Queens Court	14 E15
Mossgiel Place	14 F17	Queens Quadrant	14 F14
Mossgiel Road	14 F17	Queens Terrace	14 D15
Mosside Road	13 H11	Queens Terrace Lane	14 D15
Mote, The	17 F23	Racecourse Road	14 D17
Mount, The	17 G19	Racecourse View	14 D18
Mount Charles Crescent	16 C21	Railway Cottages	16 E22
Mountcharles	16 C21	Raithill	17 G22
Mount Oliphant Crescent	14 F17	Recawr Park	17 G20
Mount Oliphant Place	15 G17	Renwick Way	13 J10
Murchie Drive	13 J10	Rigwoodie Place	16 D22
Murdoch's Lone	16 D22	River Ayr Walk	15 J15, G16
Murray Place	13 H12	River Street	14 E14
Murray Street	13 H13	River Terrace	14 E14
Nelson Place	12 F13	Riverside Place	14 F15
New Road	12 E13	Robertson Crescent	15 J14
New Bridge Street	14 E14	Robsland Avenue	14 E18
Newark Crescent	17 A22	Rockrose Park	17 G20
Newmarket Street	14 E15	Roman Road	17 H19
Newton Park Court	12 G13	Ronaldshaw Park	14 D17
Nile Court	14 E15	Rosebank Crescent	14 E18
Nisbet Drive	13 J10	Rosebay Park	17 G21
Noltmire Road	13 H11	Ross Street	12 G13
Northdoon Place	16 C20	Rosslyn Place	12 G12
Northfield Avenue	12 F12	Rowan Crescent	15 H18
Northfield Court	12 F12	Rowallan Court (2)	14 D14
Northfield Place	12 F12	Rozelle Terrace	17 G22
North Harbour Street	14 E14	Rush Hill	17 H21
Northpark Avenue	12 G12	Russell Drive	12 F13
Nursery Grove	15 G18	Russell Street	14 F14
Nursery Road	15 G18	St Andrew's Street	14 E15
Nursery Wynd	15 G18	St Catherines Road	13 L13
Nurseryhall	13 J13	St Georges Road	12 G12
Oakwood Avenue	13 K13	St John Street	14 E14
Obree Avenue	13 J10	St Leonards Court	14 F18
Old Bridge Road	13 K12	St Leonard's Road	14 E18
Old Bridge Street	14 E14	St Leonards Wynd	14 E18
Old Farm Road	13 J12	St Phillans Avenue	15 G17
Old Hillfoot Road	15 G18	St Vincent Crescent	17 F21
Orchard Avenue	15 G17	Saltfield Lane	12 E13
Orchard House	15 G17	Saltpans Road	12 E12
Orchard Place	15 G17	Sandgate	14 E15
Oswald Court	12 F12	Sandyhill Road	15 K17
Oswald Lane	12 D13	Sandyhill Terrace	15 K17
Oswald Place	12 F10	Sannox Place	13 J13
		Sannox View	13 K13
		Sanquhar Farm Road	13 J12

Street	Grid	Street	Grid
Savoy Court	14 D16	Union Arcade	14
Savoy Park	14 D16	Union Avenue	12
Scaur o'Doon Road	16 B20	Upper Crofts	16
Sea Tower Court	14 D17	Upper Loaning	17
Sea Tower Gardens	14 D17	Victoria Park	14
Seabank Road	14 D14	Victoria Street	14
Seafield Crescent	14 C17	Viewfield Court	12
Seafield Drive	14 C18	Viewfield Road	12
Seafield Road	14 D17	Virginia Gardens	12
Seaforth Crescent	12 G11	Waggon Road	12 E
Seaforth Road	12 G11	Walker Road	12 G
Semple Road	13 J10	Wallacetown Drive	13 H
Shalloch Park	17 A21	Ward Court	12 G
Shanter Place	16 D22	Ward Road	12 G
Shanter Way	16 D22	Waterloo Road	12 G
Shanter Wynd	16 D22	Wattfield Road	14 E
Shavin Brae	15 J17	Weaver Street	12 E
Shawfield Avenue	17 F19	Weir Road	12 E
Shiel Hill	17 G21	Wellington Lane	14 D
Shieling Park	14 D16	Wellington Square	14 D
Shillilaw Drive	13 J10	Wellington Street	12 G
Shillilaw Place	13 J10	Wellpark	16 E
Shore Road	12 E12	West Place	17 F
Skye Square	14 F15	West Sanquhar Avenue	12 G
Slaphouse	16 E19	West Sanquhar Place	12 G
Sloan Street	13 J13	West Sanquhar Road	12 G
Sloan Place	13 J13	Westfield Road	14 D
Smith Street	14 E16	Westwood Avenue	15 J
Snowdrop Square	17 G20	Westwood Crescent	13 K1
Somerset Gardens	12 G13	Wexford Way (7)	14 D
Somerset Road	12 G13	Wheatfield Road	14 D
Sorrel Drive	17 H20	Wheatpark Place	13 L1
Souter Place	15 G18	Wheatpark Road	13 L1
South Beach Road	14 D14	Whin Hill Road	17 G2
South Harbour Street	14 D14	White Street	12 G1
South Lodge Court	14 D17	Whiteford View	15 J1
Southfield Park	14 F18	Whitfield Drive	13 J1
Southpark Road	14 D17	Whitletts Road	15 G1
Speedwell Square	17 G20	Whitletts Court	13 K1
Springbank Road	12 G11	Whittle Road	13 H1
Springvale Park	14 E17	Willow Park	17 H1
Springvale Road	14 E17	Wills Gardens	13 H1
Spruce Park	15 J18	Wills Road	13 H1
Spur Road	12 D13	Wilson Street	12 G13
Station Road	14 F16	Windward Park	17 F22
Stewart Road	12 G11	Wood Park	17 G19
Stewartlea	14 E17	Woodend Road	17 E22
Stobhill Crescent	15 G18	Woodfield Avenue	12 F10
Stonecrop Place	17 H19	Woodfield Crescent	12 F11
Stonefield Park	16 B21	Woodfield Lane	12 G10
Strang Place	13 J10	Woodfield Road	12 F11
Strathayr Place	14 F14	Woodlands Crescent	17 G19
Strathdoon Place	16 C21	Woodlea Place	17 G21
Sunningdale Avenue	17 F20	Wrightfield Place	16 D21
Sycamore Crescent	15 J17	Wyburn Place	12 F12
Sym's Lane	14 F14	York Place	12 E13
Taran Walk	14 F15	York Street	12 E13
Taybank Drive	17 F20	York Street Lane	12 E13
Taylor Court	12 E13	Young Street	12 G10
Taylor Street	12 E13		
Teviot Street	12 G12	**Index to Irvine**	
Thistle Street	17 H20		
Thomson Street	13 H13	Aberfeldy Terrace	43 J3
Thorneyflat Crescent	13 L13	Aberlour Place	42 H3
Thorneyflat Place	13 L13	Aberlour Road	42 H3
Thornyflat Drive	13 K13	Academy Court	44 D6
Thornyflat Road	13 K13	Academy Gardens	41 D5
Thornyflat Street	13 K13	Academy Road	44 D6
Thornwood Avenue	13 K13	Adams Walk	45 G7
Tig Road	12 F12	Afton Court	44 D7
Treebank Crescent	15 H18	Ailsa Road	44 D10
Trefoil Place	17 H20	Alder Green	43 J5
Trenchard Court (3)	14 D14	Alexander Place	41 E5
Tryfield Place	12 F13	Alford Place	42 G4
Tweed Street	12 G11		

Allan Square 45 G6
Anderson Drive 42 F4
Annandale Way 43 J4
Annick Court 44 D7
Annick Drive 46 K8
Annick Road 46 K8
(Dreghorn)
Annick Road 45 F7, G8
(Irvine)
Annick View 45 G7
Archers Avenue 42 G3
Archers Court 42 G3
Ardbeg Court 42 H3
Ardmore Court 43 J3
Arkwright Way 45 H6
Arran Place 41 D4
Arranview Court 44 D6
Ashgrove 41 E4
Auchenharvie Place 42 H3
Avon Court 43 J5
Ayr Road 45 E8, E10
Balgray Way 43 J3
Ballot Road 45 E6
Bank Court 42 G5
Bank Place 42 G5
Bank Street 45 E6, 42 G5
Bankhead Avenue 47 Q6
Barbeth Place 43 J4
Barclay Gardens 43 M3
Barony Court 42 H5
Barr Crescent 41 E5
Barra Crescent 46 L7
Barra Lane 46 L7
Barra Place 46 L7
Barra Wynd 46 L7
Bartonholm Gardens 41 B3
Beach Drive 44 B8
Beaton Terrace 41 E4
Beech Avenue 45 F7
Belfast Quay 44 C7
Bell Crescent 42 F4
Benbain Place 43 K3
Bencleuch Place 46 K6
Bensley Avenue 42 H4
Bensley Rise 42 H4
Benthill Terrace 44 C8
Beresford Grove 42 G4
Berry Drive 45 G6
Berryhill Avenue 43 K3
Bilby Terrace 41 E4
Bimson Place 44 C8
Bimson Row 44 C8
Birks Hill 43 J5
Birkscairn Place 46 L7
Birkscairn Way 46 L7
Blairdenon Way 46 K7
Blaven Head 43 J5
Bodesbeck Court 46 J6
Bonnyton Place 43 J4
Bonnyton Row 43 J4
Bowhouse Head 43 K4
Bowhouse Rise 43 K4
Bowmore Court 43 J3
Boyle Street 44 C7
Bradbury Glebe 45 E7
Braefoot 42 H4
Braehead 42 H4
Braeside 42 H4
Brewster Place 45 H10
Bryce Knox Court 43 J3
Bridgegate 45 E7
Broomlands 45 G7, 46 K7
Busway
Broomlands Court 46 J7
Broomlands Drive 45 F7

Broomlands Gate 46 J7
Broomlands Place 45 F7
Broomlands Road 46 K8
Broughton Green 43 K3
Brown Walk 42 F4
Bruce Terrace 42 F4
Burnbrae Crescent 43 L3
Burnbrae Drive 43 L3
Burns Crescent 43 J4
Burns Street 44 D6
Burnside Place 41 D5
Busbiehead (2) 43 K4
Bute Court 46 L8
Cairngorm Court 43 K4
Cairnmount Road 42 H2
Cairnsgarroch Way 46 K7
Cairnsmore Way 46 K7
Caldon Road 42 F5
Campbell Place 46 K9
Campsie Avenue 46 K6
Campsie Walk 46 K6
Campsie Way 46 J7
Capel Place 46 K7
Capringstone Foot 43 K4
Cardon Place 46 K7
Cardow Crescent 43 J3
Carmel Drive 47 Q8
Carmichael Place 41 D4
Carnoustie Place 45 G10
Carrick Drive 41 D4
Carron Place 41 E3
Carson Drive 45 E9
Carters Place 45 E7
Carters Rigg 44 D8
Castle Keep Gardens 42 H5
Castle Place 44 D6
Castle Street 44 D6
Castlepark Circle 41 E3
Castlepark Crescent 41 D3
Castlepark Road 41 D3
Cedar Road 42 F5
Centenary Road 45 H10
Century Court 45 H10
Chalmers Place 49 H11
Chapel Lane 45 E7
Chapelgill Place 43 J5
Cherry Gardens 42 G4
Cheviot Court 46 J6
Cheviot Head 46 J6
Cheviot Way 46 J6
Church Street 44 D7
Clark Drive 45 F7, 42 G5
Clayton Avenue 41 E5
Coach Brae View 47 N7
Cochrane Street 44 D7
Cockburn Place 49 H11
Coleburn Court 42 H3
Coll Gardens 46 K9
Corse Avenue 47 Q8
Corsehill Mount 46 J8, K9
Road
Corsehill Park 47 M9
Corsehill Terrace 47 N7
Corserine Bank 46 H6
Cotton Row 45 E7
Craig View 47 Q7
Craigmark Place 42 H4
Craignaw Place 46 K7
Cramalt Court 46 J6
Cramond Place 46 H7
Cramond Way 46 H7
Craven Grove 42 H4
Crocus Grove 45 E6
Croft Terrace 47 P7
Crofthead Court 46 J6

Crofthead 46 J6
Crompton Way 45 G6
Cuillin Place 43 J5
Cumbrae Court 46 L8
Cunninghame Road 44 D9
Cypress Gardens 42 G4
Dale Crescent 42 F5
Dalgain Court 43 J4
Dalmailing Avenue 46 K8
Dalmore Place 42 H3
Dalmore Way 42 H3
Dalrymple Drive 45 F6
Dalrymple Place 45 F6
Dalwhinnie Court 42 H3
Dalrymple Court 45 G6
Darnshaw Close 43 L3
Dick Crescent 42 F4
Dick Terrace 42 F4
Dickson Drive 41 D4, 42 E4
Donaldson Drive 42 F5
Doon Court 45 E7
Doura Drive 42 H4
Doura Place 41 E4
Drumelzier Court 43 J5
Drummond Crescent 45 G10
Drumuir Foot 43 K4
Dublin Quay 44 C7
Duncan Drive 45 F7
Dundonald Road 46 L8
Dunlop Crescent 46 K8
Dunlop Drive 48 G13
Dunlop Place 49 H13
Duntonknoll 41 E5
Dunvegan Place 42 F3
Earncraig Green 46 J6
Earls Bridge Gardens 42 G2
Earls Bridge Place 42 G2
Earlswood Avenue 42 G3, G4
Earlswood View 42 G3
Earlswood Way 42 G3
Earlswood Wynd 42 G3
East Bowhouse Head 43 K4
East Bowhouse Way 43 K4
East Broomlands 46 K7
East Road 41 D1
(Ravenspark)
East Road (Irvine) 45 E6, E7
Eastwood Avenue 42 F5
Eglinton Gardens 45 E6
Eglinton Street 45 E6
Elmbank Terrace 42 F5
Eriskay Court 46 L9
Esplanade 44 B8
Etive Place 42 F4
Fairlie Drive 43 K3
Fairways, The 41 C2
Fencedyke Close 42 H5
Fencedyke Way 43 J5, 46 J6
Finnie Terrace 47 P7
Fintry Place 46 K7
Fintry Terrace 46 K6
Fintry Walk 46 K7
First Avenue 45 E9
First Street 41 D1
Fleming Terrace 41 D4
Ford Avenue 47 M8
Fortacre Place 43 K4
Frew Terrace 41 E4
Friars Croft 44 D7
Fullarton Street 45 E8
Gailes Road 48 E12, E13
Galt Avenue 45 F6
Gardens, The 43 L3
Garelet Place 46 K7
Garnock Court 45 E7

Garrier Court 47 P7
Garrier Road 47 P7
Gateside 42 H3
George Court 45 E6
George Terrace 45 E6
Gigha Crescent 46 K7
Gigha Lane 46 K7
Gigha Place 46 K7
Gigha Terrace 46 K7
Gigha Wynd 46 K7
Gilbertfield Place 45 F7
Girdle Gate 42 H4
Girdle Toll 43 J4
Glasgow Vennel 45 E7
Glebe, The 46 L8, L9
Glenbervie Wynd 45 F9
Gleneagles Place 45 G10
Glenleith Place 46 L7
Glenlyon Grove 42 H4
Goldcraig Court 43 J4
Golf Place 41 D4
Golffields Road 45 F8
Gottries Place 44 C8
Gottries Road 44 C8
Grampian Court 43 K5
Grange, The 43 L3
Gray Crescent 45 E9
Green Avenue 41 E5
Greenbank Court 45 E8
Greenbank Road 45 E8
Greenfield Drive 45 F7
Greenhill Court 43 K3
Greenside 43 J5
Greenside Avenue 47 Q8
Greenside Terrace 47 Q7
Greenside Way 43 J5
Greenwood Gate 46 J8
Greenwood Road 46 L8
Gullane Court 45 F9
Gulliland Place 45 F8
Haddington Gardens 43 K3
Harbour Road 44 C8
Harbour Street 44 C8
Harris Court 46 L9
Harris Terrace 46 L9
Heatherhouse Road 44 D9
Heatherstane Bank 46 L7
Heatherstane Walk 46 K7
Heatherstane Way 46 L7
Heathfield House 44 D6
Hepburn Way 43 L2
Herbertson Crescent 42 F5
High Street 45 E7
Highet Gardens 41 D5
Highfield Place 42 H3
Hill Street 45 E7
Hillshaw Foot 46 L7
Hillshaw Green 46 L7
Holms Avenue 47 M8
Hopetoun Bank 46 L7
Howat Crescent 45 G6
Hunter Drive 41 D3
Inverleven Place 42 H2
Iona Court 46 L9
Iona Place 46 L9
Irvine Mains Crescent 41 E5
Irvine Road 41 C1
Islay Court 46 L9
James Crescent 41 E5
Jermond Drive 42 F4
Jura Court 46 L9
Kames Court 43 K3
Katrine Place 42 F3
Kennedy Park 46 K9
Kerr Drive 45 F7

Kerr Place	45 F7	MacKinnon Terrace	42 G5
Kersland Foot	42 H4	MacKintosh Place	45 H8
Kidsneuk	41 C3	Macredie Place	43 M3
Kidsneuk Gardens	41 C3	MacRobert Avenue	46 K8
Killoch Place	42 H5	McClure Gardens	45 E6
Killoch Way	42 H5	McDonald Drive	42 F5
Kilmarnock Road	47 Q7	McGibney Drive	45 F8
Kiln Court	45 E7	McKinlay Crescent	44 D8
Kiln Walk	45 E7	McLean Drive	47 M9
Kilpatrick Court	46 J6	McMillan Place	49 H11
Kilpatrick Place	46 J7	Malcolm Gardens	45 F7
Kilsyth Crescent	46 J6	Maid Morville Avenue	46 L9
Kilsyth Walk	46 J6	Main Road	47 P7
Kilwinning Road	41 C2, D5	Main Street	46 L8
Kirk Vennel	45 E7	Mansfield Way	43 J4
Kirkgate	45 E7	Manson Road	42 G5
Kirkhill	43 L3	Manuel Court	46 L9
Kirkland Terrace	47 P7	Manuel Terrace	46 L9
Kirkstyle Court	43 K3	Maple Terrace	42 F5
Knockentiber Road	47 Q7	Marble Avenue	47 M8
Kyle Avenue	47 P7	Maree Place	42 F2
Kyle Road	44 D9, D10	Marine Drive	44 C9, 48 D11
Ladyacre Avenue	42 F3	Marress Road	44 D6
Ladyacre Court	42 G3	Martin Avenue	42 F4
Ladyacre Place	42 G3	Maxwell Green	43 J5
Ladyacre Way	42 F3	Maxwood Place	43 J4
Ladyacre Wynd	42 F3	Meadow Avenue	41 E5
Ladyburn Court	42 H3	Meadowhead	48 G13
Ladyha Court	43 K4	Avenue	
Lamberton Gardens	43 L4	Meadowhead	49 H12, H14
Lammermuir Court	46 J6	Road	
Lamont Drive	45 E9	Meadows, The	41 D5
Lamont Place	45 E9	Meikle Place	43 K3
Lanfine Row	43 J3	Merrick Place	46 K7
Lanfine Terrace	42 H3	Merryvale Road	45 E8
Lanfine Way	43 J3	Metcalfe Place	49 H11
Langmuir Avenue	43 L4	Mid Rig	43 J5
Langmuir Court	43 L4	Middleton Park	43 J5
Lawers Place	43 J5	Middleton Road	43 J5
Lawthorn Road	43 K3	Milgarholm Avenue	45 F8
Leven Place	42 F3	Mill Crescent	45 G7
Lewis Court	46 J7	Mill Road	45 F7
Lewis Crescent	46 H7	Millbank Row	47 M8
Lewis Rise	46 J7	Millburn Terrace	43 J3
Lewis Terrace	46 J7	Milldown Place	46 L7
Lewis Wynd	46 J7	Millfore Court	46 J6
Linkwood Court	43 J3	Milton Court	47 M8
Linkwood Place	43 J3	Milton Crescent	46 L8
Linthouse Vennel	44 C8	Milton Road	46 L8
Lismore Drive	46 K9	Monach Gardens	46 K9
Lismore Way	46 K9	Montgomery Lane	44 D8
Littlestane Court	43 J3	Montgomery Place	44 C8
Littlestane Rise	43 J3	Montgomery Street	44 C8
Littlestane Road	43 J3	Montgomeryfield	46 K9
Littlestane Row	43 J3	Moorfoot Place	46 J6
Livingstone Terrace	41 E4	Moorfoot Way	46 J6
Loach Avenue	45 F8	Morar Place	41 E3
Lochcraig Court	46 J6	Moss Drive	48 G12
Lochlibo Court	43 J3	Mossgiel Drive	45 F6
Lochlibo Road	42 H4, 43 J1	Mount View	46 L8
Lochwood Place	42 H3	Muir Drive	45 F6
Lomond Place	42 F3	Muirfield Court	45 G10
Lomond Way	43 J5	Muirhall Place	46 L8
Long Drive	42 F2, 49 J12	Mull Court	46 J7
Longrow Gardens	42 H2	Mull Crescent	46 J7
Loudoun Rigg	45 E8	Mull Place	46 J7
Low Green Road	44 D6	Mull Terrace	46 J7
Lower Vennel (1)	46 J6	Murchland Way	41 E5
Lowther Bank	46 L7	Murdoch Place	49 H11
Lugar Avenue	43 J3	Neil Avenue	42 F4
Lugton Court	45 E7	Nevis Way	43 J5
Lyle Gardens	45 F8	New Street	44 D7
MacAdam Place	45 H8	Newfield Place	43 K4
MacAllan Place	42 H2	Newhouse Way	43 J4
MacAra Drive	45 G6	Newtonhead (1)	43 K4

Norman Crescent	41 D4	Seagate	44 D6
North Vennel	46 J6	Seaton Terrace	41 E4
Nursery Gardens	47 Q7	Second Avenue	44 D9
Oaklands Avenue	42 E5	Shalloch Place	46 K7
Ochil Court	43 J4	Sharpe Avenue	47 M9
Old Caley Road	41 E4, E5	Shawholm Gardens	45 E6
Ormiston Place	43 L2	Shiel Place	41 E3
Overton Place	43 K4	Shielhope Court	43 J5
Overtoun Court	47 P7	Sidlaw Foot	46 L7
Overtoun Road	47 P6	Sillars Meadow	45 G7
Paddock, The	43 L3	Skye Court	46 K9
Park Place	41 D4	Slate Mill Gardens	45 G7
Parkside	46 K6	Sloan Avenue	45 F
Parterre	45 E7	Smiddy Close	45
Paterson Avenue	42 F4, F5	Smith Avenue	42
Paterson Crescent	42 F4	Smithstone Court	42
Pavilion Gardens	42 G3	Smithstone Way	42
Peden Place	45 E7	Somerville Park	43
Penbreck Court	43 K4	Somerville Way	43
Pennant Court	42 G2	Sophia Crescent	41
Pennant Place	42 G2	Sourlie Terrace	42
Pennant Way	42 G2	Southook Row	43
Pennyvenie Way	43 J4	South Newmoor	45 G8,
Pentland Place	46 J6	Avenue	
Perceton Row	47 M6	South Vennel (2)	46
Peter Street	44 C8	Speyburn Place	42
Piersland Place	43 J4	Springbank Gardens	43
Pladda Avenue	46 J7	Springfield Gardens	43
Pladda Court	46 K7	Springhill Terrace	47
Pladda Crescent	46 J7	Springside Terrace	47
Pladda Terrace	46 K7	Staffa Court	46
Pladda Wynd	46 K7	Stanecastle Drive	42
Portland Avenue	44 D9	Stanecastle Gate	42
Portland Place	44 D9	Stanecastle Road	42
Portland Road	44 C9	Station Brae	46
Puddle Ford	45 E7	Station Brae Gardens	46
Purdies Close	45 E7	Station Drive	47
Quarry Road	45 E7	Station Road	47
Queen Road	41 E4	Steadman Place	46
Queen's Court	45 F7	Steps Road	42 E
Racecourse Place	41 C4	Stewart Drive	42 F
Ramstane Place	43 L3	Strathmore Park	43 K
Ranken Crescent	45 F6	Stroma Court	46 L
Ranken Drive	45 F6	Stronsay Court	46 J
Rannoch Place	41 D2	Stronsay Way	46 J
(Ravenspark)		Swinton Place	43 K
Rannoch Place	41 E3	Symington Place	45 H11
(Irvine)		Tarryholme Drive	45 E
Ravenscroft	41 D4	Telford Place	45 H
Redburn Gate	41 C2	Third Avenue	44 D9
Redburn Place	41 D4	Thornhouse Avenue	45 F
Regalia View	42 G3	Thornhouse Court	45 F
Renton Park	43 L2	Thornwood Drive	45 E
Rig Foot	43 K4	Tiree Court	46 K9
Riverside Avenue	46 J10	Titchfield Way	43 J4
Riverside Road	47 M8	Tollerton Drive	42 F5
Riverside Way	45 H9	Tollhouse Way	43 J4
Riverway	44 D8	Towerlands	42 H5, 46 K7
Ronaldsay Court	46 K9	Farm Road	
Rosebank Gardens	42 H2	Towerlands Gate	46 K7
Roseholm Avenue	45 G7	Towerlands	46 J6, 47 N7
Rowan Terrace	42 F5	Road	
Rowantree Gardens	43 J4	Townfoot	46 K9
Rubie Crescent	45 E9	Townfoot Lane	46 K8
St Andrews Way	45 F9	Townhead	45 F7
St Bride's Place	41 E4	Turnberry Wynd	45 F9
St Inan Avenue	45 G6	Victoria Crescent	44 D8
St Kilda Bank	46 J7	Vineburgh Avenue	41 E5
St Kilda Court	46 J7	Vineburgh Court	41 D5
St Kilda Place	46 J7	Vines, The	41 E5
Sanderson Avenue	44 D8	Wallace Road	41 E5
Sandy Road	41 B2, C4	Wardlaw Gardens	43 K2
Sandy Road Place	41 B3	Wardneuk Court	43 J3
School Lane	45 E8	Warrix Avenue	45 F8
Scott Road	45 E8	Warwick Hill	43 K4

Watercut Road 41 B1, C1
Waterside 44 D6
Watson Terrace 45 F7
Weavers Wynd 45 E6
West Bowhouse 43 J4
 Gardens
West Bowhouse Head 43 J4
West Bowhouse Way 43 J4
West Court 44 D7
West Road 41 D2
 (Ravenspark)
West Road 44 D6, D7
 (Irvine)
 hitehope Green 43 J5
 hitewisp Court 43 J5
 hittle Place 45 H7
 hyte Avenue 45 F8
 lliam Burns Place 46 L8
 lliamfield Park 41 D5
 lliamfield Grove 41 D5
 llow Gardens 42 G4
 ilson Avenue 42 E5
 indelstraw Court 46 J6
 inton Place 41 E5
 ood Grove 46 L8
 oodhill Crescent 43 K3
 oodlands Avenue 45 F6
 yvis Place 43 J5

dex to Kilwinning

 bbey View 62 B3
 bbeygate 63 E4
 bbeygreen 63 E4
 bbot's Avenue 63 E5
 bbot's Place 63 E4
 bbot's Walk 63 E4
 insdale Court 62 B4
 lexandra Gardens 62 D4
 lexandra Terrace 62 D4
 lmswall Road 63 E4
 nnanhill Place 62 B4
 rdmillan 62 B5
 shgrove Road 62 C3
 tholl Gardens 63 E3
 uchenkist Place 62 D2
 aberton Way 62 B4
 aird Avenue 63 E3
 ankhead Road 63 F4
 annoch Cottages 63 G2
 annoch Gardens 63 G3
 annoch Place 63 G4
 annoch Road 63 G2
 argeny 62 B5
 artonholm Terrace 63 F6
 eechwood 62 D2
 elleisle Close 62 C3
 evan Gardens 63 E3
 irkdale Court 62 C3
 irklands Wynd 62 B3
 Blacklands Avenue 63 E5
 Blacklands Crescent 63 E6
 Blair Road 63 F3
 Blairafton Wynd 62 C2
 Braid Court 62 B4
 Braidwood Road 63 E3
 Bridgend Lane 63 F4
 Bridgend Pathfoot 63 F4
 Brodick Avenue 62 C3
 Brodick Close 62 C3
 Broomfield Street 63 E2
 Broomhill Court 62 C2
 Bruntsfield Avenue 62 B4
 Burns Place 63 F4
 Busby Place 63 F3

Byrehill Avenue 63 E5
 (Blacklands)
Byrehill Avenue 62 B5
 (W Byrehill)
Byrehill Drive 62 A5
Byrehill Place 62 B5
Byrehill Road 62 D6
Byres Loch 62 D4
Byres Road 62 D4
Calderwood 63 E2
Cambusdoon Place 62 D4
Carnoustie Court 62 B4
Cartle Close 62 C1
Cartleburn Gardens 62 D2
Cassiland Place 62 B3
Castlehill Farm 62 A4
Cathkin Place 62 B3
Chalybeate Court 62 D4
Church Street 63 E4
Churchill Avenue 63 F3
Claremont Crescent 62 D3
Clonbeith Court 62 D2
Cloncaird 62 C5
Coodham Place 62 D4
Corsehill 63 G4
Cranberry Court 62 C4
Cranberry Head 62 C4
Cranberry Moss 62 C6, D4
 Road
Cranberry Place 62 C4
Cranberry Road 62 B5
Crannog Way 62 C3
Culzean Place 62 C5
Dalgarven Wynd 62 C2
Daljarrock 62 B5
Dalmahoy Way 62 B4
Dalry Road 62 D2
Darmule Drive 62 C2
David Gage Street 63 E2
Davids Crescent 62 D5
Deanfield Court 63 E4
Dirrans Terrace 63 F5
Dornoch Court 62 B4
Dovecot Lane 63 F4
Druid Drive 63 E3
Dubbs Road 62 A6
Duddingston Avenue 62 B3
Dunure Courts 62 D4
Eden Court 62 B4
Edison Place 63 E6
Edzell Row 62 B4
Eglinton Place 63 E4
Enterkine 62 B5
Evelyn-Terrace 62 D5
Fairhaven Square 62 B3
Fergushill Road 63 F4
Five Roads 63 G4
Forge Vennel 62 C3
Foundry Court 62 C3
Foundry Wynd 62 C3
Friars Lawn 62 D4
Gagarin Terrace 63 E5
Ganton Court 62 B4
Garden Lane 63 E4
Garden Square 63 E4
Garnock View 63 E3
Garrallan 62 C5
Glebe Street 63 E3
Glenapp Court 62 C5
Glenapp Place 62 C5
Glenbervie Drive 62 B4
Glenburn Close 62 C1
Gleneagles Avenue 62 C3
Graystones 63 E2
Greenfoot 63 E4

Groatholm Way 62 D2
Gullane Place 62 B4
Hamilton Court 63 E3
Hamilton Street 63 E3
Hawthorn Place 63 E5
Hawthorn Court 63 E5
Hazeldene Park 63 F3
Hazel Grove 63 G3
Helen's Terrace 63 E5
Heronswood 62 D2
Highfield Street 63 F3
Hillcrest Place 63 F4
Hillpark Rise 62 B4
Howden Avenue 63 E3
Howgate 62 D4
Hoylake Square 62 C3
Hunter Place 63 G4
Innerwood Road 63 E2
Irvine Road 63 F5
James Clements 62 C3
 Close
Keir Hardie Crescent 63 G4
Kelburne 62 C5
Kelvin Avenue 63 F6
Kilkerran 62 C4
Killermont Place 62 B4
Kilrig Avenue 63 E3
King Street 63 E3
Kinnis Vennel 62 C3
Kirkhill 62 C5
Kyleswell Street 63 E4
Ladyacre 63 E3
Ladyford Avenue 63 E4
Lainshaw 62 C5
Lauchlan Way 63 E4
Lissens Walk 62 C2
Lochwood Close 62 C2
Longford Avenue 63 E6
Loudoun Crescent 62 B3
Love Street 63 G4
McGavin Avenue 63 G4
McGavin Way 62 D3
McLuckie Drive 62 C4
McLuckie Park 62 C3
Machrie Place 62 C4
Main Street 63 E4, F4
Manse Court 63 E4
Matthew Place 63 E2
Meadows, The 62 D3
Meadow Park Road 62 C3
Meadow View 62 C2
Meadow Way 62 C2
Millside Gardens 63 F4
Moncur Court 62 C2
Moncur Road 63 G4
Monkreddan Crescent 62 C2
Montgomerie Terrace 63 G4
Montgreenan View 63 F4
Morville Crescent 63 E2
Mountcastle Wynd 62 C1
Muirfield Place 62 C3
Muirside Court 62 C5
Muirside Place 62 C5
Muirside Road 62 C5
Muirside Steadings 62 A5
Nairn Court 62 B4
Nethermains 63 E5, E6
 Road
Newark 62 C5
Ninian's Terrace 63 F5
Northacre 63 E2
Northacre Grove 62 D2
Nursery Drive 62 C2
Nursery Wynd 62 C2
Old Glasgow Road 63 G3

Old Woodwynd Road 62 D3
Orchard Grove 63 E3
Orchard Place 63 E3
Oxenward Road 63 E4
Park Avenue 63 E4
Park Lane 62 D2
Parkhead Avenue 63 F4
Pathfoot View 63 F4
Papingo Close 62 C1
Pennyburn Road 62 D4, B5
Pinmore 62 C5
Pollock Crescent 63 E5
Prestonfield Avenue 62 B3
Priory Wynd 62 C1, C2
Queen Street 63 G4
Queens Place 63 G4
Redstone Avenue 63 F3
River Walk 63 E2
Robert W Service 63 E5
 Court
Rosemount 62 C5
Rowallan 62 C5
St Winning's 62 D4, 63 E4
 Road
St Winning's Lane 63 E4
St Winning's Well 62 D4
St Joan's Crescent 63 E5
Segton Avenue 62 C4
Seymour Avenue 63 F5
Shavian Terrace 63 E5
Simpson Place 63 F6
Skelmorlie Place 62 D4
Smiddy Court 63 E4
Smith Crescent 63 F5
Station Plaza 62 D4
Stevenston Road 62 B4
Stobbs Crescent 63 E5
Stobbs Terrace 63 E5
Sundrum Place 62 D5
Sunningdale Square 62 C3
Sutton Court 62 B4
Tammy Dale's Road 63 F4
Thornhill Court 62 B4
Townhead 62 D3
Treesbank 62 C5
Turnberry Court 62 B4
Underwood 62 D3
Vaults Lane 63 E4
Viaduct Circle 63 E2
Wallwood 62 C5
Waterside Road 63 E3
Weirston Road 63 G4
Wentworth Square 62 C3
West Doura Court 62 B4
West Doura Way 62 C4
Whitehirst Park Road 62 B3
Winstanley Wynd 62 C2
Winton Avenue 62 C4
Wood Crescent 63 E3
Wood Street 63 E3
Woodburn Avenue 63 E3
Woodfarm Close 62 D1
Woodgreen Wynd 62 C2
Woodmill 63 F6
Woodside Road 62 C1, C3
Woodwynd 63 E3